Bipartisanship and the Making of Foreign Policy: A Historical Survey

---

Bipartisanship and the Making of Foreign Policy: A Historical Survey

EDITED BY
Ellen C. Collier

Routledge
Taylor & Francis Group
LONDON AND NEW YORK

First published 1991 by Westview Press

Published 2018 by Routledge
52 Vanderbilt Avenue, New York, NY 10017
2 Park Square, Milton Park, Abingdon, Oxon OX14 4RN

Routledge is an imprint of the Taylor & Francis Group, an informa business

Copyright © 1991 by Taylor & Francis

All rights reserved. No part of this book may be reprinted or reproduced or utilised in any form or by any electronic, mechanical, or other means, now known or hereafter invented, including photocopying and recording, or in any information storage or retrieval system, without permission in writing from the publishers.

Notice:
Product or corporate names may be trademarks or registered trademarks, and are used only for identification and explanation without intent to infringe.

Library of Congress Cataloging-in-Publication Data
Bipartisanship and the making of foreign policy : a historical survey
 / edited by Ellen C. Collier.
   p. cm.
  ISBN 0-8133-8149-5
  1. United States—Foreign relations administation—History.
2. Executive power—United States—History.   3. Legislative power—
United States—History.   I. Collier, Ellen C. (Ellen Oodfelter),
1927–   .
JX1706.B57   1991
353.0089—dc20   91-7172
                                                                            CIP

ISBN 13: 978-0-367-01613-5 (hbk)
ISBN 13: 978-0-367-16600-7 (pbk)

To Ed--
marriage teaches bipartisanship.

Contents

List of Tables xi
Preface xiii

PART ONE
BIPARTISAN FOREIGN POLICY AND POLICYMAKING
SINCE WORLD WAR II

1 Introduction 3

2 **Meanings of Bipartisan Foreign Policy** 5

   Agreement on Substance of Policy, 5
   Policymaking Process, 11

3 **Postwar Record of Bipartisanship** 19

   Early Postwar Bipartisan Foreign Policy Model:
      Building Consensus, 19
   Areas Lacking Consensus, 24
   Fresh Effort at Bipartisan Foreign Policy, 35

4 **Perspectives on Bipartisan Foreign Policy** 41

   Bipartisanship for Strength and Continuity, 41
   Cautions on Bipartisanship:
      Need for Criticism and Accountability, 42
   Bipartisanship When Helpful, 44

5 Issues   45

Roles of President and Congress in Foreign Policy, 45
Source of Differences on Foreign Policy, 48
Uniqueness of Foreign Policy, 51
The Partisan Context: Can Foreign Policy
  Be Separated from Politics? 52

6 Building a Bipartisan Foreign Policy   55

Techniques of a Bipartisan Foreign Policy, 55
Attitudinal Requirements, 64

7 Conclusion   67

NOTES TO PART ONE, 69

PART TWO
DOCUMENTS ON BIPARTISAN FOREIGN POLICYMAKING

Models of Making Bipartisan Foreign Policy   79

Charter of the United Nations; Report of the Senate Foreign
  Relations Committee, July 16, 1945 (Excerpts), 79
European Recovery Program; Report of the Senate Foreign
  Relations Committee, February 27, 1948 (Excerpts), 85
North Atlantic Treaty; Report of the Senate Foreign
  Relations Committee, June 6, 1949 (Excerpts), 92
Japanese Peace Treaty and Other Treaties Relating to
  Security in the Pacific; Report of the Senate Foreign
  Relations Committee, February 14, 1952 (Excerpts), 98
Bipartisan Accord on Central America, March 24, 1989, 102

The Importance of Criticism   105

Constructive Criticism of Foreign Policy Is Essential
  to the Safety of the Nation; Remarks by Senator
  Robert Taft, January 5, 1951 (Excerpt), 105

Southeast Asia Resolution; Dissenting Remarks by Senator
   Wayne Morse, August 6, 1954 (Excerpts), 110
The Dominican Republic; Comments by Senator William
   Fulbright, October 22, 1965 (Excerpts), 115
Notes, 118

PART THREE
STRENGTHENING EXECUTIVE-LEGISLATIVE
CONSULTATION ON FOREIGN POLICY
House Foreign Affairs Committee Print, October 1983, Excerpt

Foreword 123

Preface 125

Principal Findings 127

Part 1: The Meaning of Consultation 135

Part 2: Problems in the Consultation Process 151

Part 3: Improving Consultation 175

Tables

1	Presidents, Party Majorities, and Foreign Policy Support in Congress Since 1947	13
2	Patterns of Bipartisan and Partisan Voting	14

Tables

Preface

Bipartisan foreign policymaking has almost become a lost art. It flourished for a short period at the end of World War II, but since that time has been rare. The executive and legislative branches and both major political parties in the United States have cooperated and compromised for short periods on foreign policy when necessary to achieve specific purposes. Yet in recent years they have seldom made concerted efforts from the outset of a new international problem to develop a bipartisan policy.

After the initial post World War II period, Presidents seemed less willing to bring Congress into the formulation of policies at an early stage. The decline in efforts at bipartisan foreign policymaking became apparent during the Korean War. Later, the Vietnam War served as a watershed in legislative-executive relations that heightened distrust between the branches and convinced Congress of the need to reassert its power in foreign policy. In addition, recurrent divided government, in which the President belongs to one party and the majority of Congress belongs to the other, gave many legislative-executive conflicts a partisan tone.

Few observers dispute the success of the early bipartisan planning that began with the United Nations and continued through the Marshall Plan and the North Atlantic Treaty and other regional security treaties. Because those core foreign policies endured with strong support for many years, it seems fruitful to reexamine the methods by which they were developed. In the past some observers have contended that past methods would not work because it was a unique set of circumstances at the end of the Second World War, not the mode of policymaking, that fostered basic consensus. Now changes in the

Soviet Union and other world events have brought a new set of comparable circumstances. Now as then a unique situation exists in which old policies are clearly outdated and new policies are required. The situation warrants efforts to create a new post-Cold War foreign policy with the same deliberation that occurred at the end of the Second World War.

Even before the transformation of Eastern Europe, at the beginning of 1989 both executive branch leaders and Members of Congress called for renewed efforts at bipartisanship in foreign policy. They remembered bitter legislative-executive disputes in the Reagan Administration that impeded unified and consistent policies in such areas as Central America and South Africa. A brief glimmer of the potential reappeared with the bipartisan accord on Central America in March 1989.

Calls for a bipartisan foreign policy often evoke varying reactions. Some view the desirability of a foreign policy supported by both political parties as self-evident on grounds that it provides strength and continuity. Others contend that the phrase has been used to stifle criticism and cloud accountability for a policy. Such different reactions are not surprising because the term "bipartisan foreign policy" has many meanings, and experience has revealed both strengths and weaknesses. The challenge is to develop a bipartisan policy without dampening criticism or closing the policy to revision.

Part I of this book examines the various meanings and reviews the history of bipartisan foreign policymaking since World War II. It explores major issues involved including the appropriate roles for the President and Congress in foreign policy, whether policy differences follow party lines, and whether politics can or should be separated from foreign policy any more than from domestic policy. It also reviews techniques used for making a bipartisan foreign policy. The study was prepared as a report for Congress published by the Congressional Research Service of the Library of Congress.

Part II presents documents relating to bipartisan foreign policy. One group, models of making bipartisan foreign policy, includes excerpts from congressional committee reports showing how policy was made on the United Nations Charter, the European Recovery Program, the North Atlantic Treaty, and the

Japanese Peace Treaty. Also included as a model is the 1989 bipartisan agreement on Central America. A second group contains excerpts from three speeches on the Senate floor that illustrate the importance of criticism and the pressure Members may feel not to criticize a foreign policy that is called bipartisan.

Part III discusses legislative-executive consultation on foreign policy, one of the key components of a bipartisan foreign policy. The study examines the continuing lack of adequate consultation of Congress by the executive, the apparent barriers to consultation, and options that both the legislative and executive branches might take to strengthen consultation. This was the final report in a series of studies on consultation published by the House Foreign Affairs Committee. Its preface further describes the consultation project and acknowledges the many people involved.

Ellen C. Collier

PART ONE

Bipartisan Foreign Policy and Policymaking Since World War II

(Adapted from a study written by Ellen C. Collier and published by the Congressional Research Service, Library of Congress, November 9, 1989, as a CRS Report for Congress.)

1

Introduction

Recently a new set of foreign and domestic conditions has led many to call for a new bipartisan foreign policy. Abroad, many of the circumstances on which the original post-World War II bipartisan foreign policy was based have been altered. At home, legislative-executive conflicts have frequently been seen as impeding effective foreign policymaking.

First, at the international level, basic changes have occurred that, for some observers, make many U.S. policies obsolete or inadequate. Suddenly the Cold War virtually ended as Soviet President Gorbachev introduced policies of economic restructuring, openness leading to more political freedom, and new thinking in international relations symbolized by the withdrawal of Soviet forces from Afghanistan in 1988. The new Soviet policies spilled over into Eastern Europe and led to a new Europe with a reunited Germany. More gradually, the United States relatively declined from the preeminent economic and technological position it had at the end of the Second World War as Western Europe and Japan prospered and newly industrialized nations emerged in Asia and Latin America. Environmental degradation, illegal narcotics, and international terrorism became national security concerns different from but, to many, no less real than the threat of aggression by the Soviet Union was in 1947.

Second, at the domestic level, the United States has a divided government, with the majority of the 101st Congress belonging to a different party than the President. Although cooperation between the two branches and parties is important for effective action, a pattern persists in which even a very popular President is often unable to carry Congress and congressional actions are often not able to secure White House support. While the same circumstance existed throughout most of the 1980s, the latter half of the decade brought new motivation for change as divisiveness and contention increasingly hampered the United States in maintaining strong and effective foreign policy in some areas, particularly Central America.

Not all observers or political practitioners agree that a bipartisan foreign policy is desirable. Moreover, they may be talking about different things when they speak of one. The first section of this paper explores the various meanings of bipartisan foreign policy. The second section traces the history of bipartisan foreign policy from its post-World War II peak through its decline since the Korean War and recent new efforts to establish a bipartisan foreign policy in certain areas. The third section presents differing perspectives on the strength and weaknesses of a bipartisan foreign policy.

The fourth section examines the issues at the heart of varying perspectives, such as the appropriate roles of the President and Congress in foreign policy, charges of congressional "micromanagement," and whether foreign policy can be bipartisan in intensely partisan surroundings. A fifth section discusses methods for developing a bipartisan foreign policy when it is deemed useful, as well as necessary attitudes. The conclusion summarizes the main findings.

2

Meanings of Bipartisan Foreign Policy

The term "bipartisan foreign policy" is not precise and is used to mean several different things. In two broad categories, it is used both for policy and process: policy which has the support of both political parties or both branches, and the process by which members of the two parties and two branches develop such a policy. Within each category the term also may have different meanings from time to time.

The term is somewhat misleading if it implies a single bipartisan U.S. foreign policy as a whole. U.S. foreign policy is comprised of many policies and programs for different geographical regions and functional problems, and may include international economic and military policy. Bipartisan foreign policies in some areas may coexist with foreign policies in other areas that would not be considered bipartisan in any sense. Almost no policy is purely partisan or bipartisan.

Agreement on Substance of Policy

At its broadest understanding, a bipartisan foreign policy means a policy on which a national consensus can be considered to exist because it has the support of both the President and Congress and both political parties. But a bipartisan foreign policy has many shades of meanings and a policy can be considered bipartisan with various levels of support from members of the two political parties. Levels of congressional support may vary from a strong bipartisan consensus to coalitions that barely get enough votes for passage.[1]

Legislative-Executive Agreement

Often the term bipartisan foreign policy does not refer to partisan support at all but is used to mean a policy that has the support of both the President and Congress, whether or not they are of the same political party. A better term in this case might be a national policy. Because under the U.S. Constitution foreign policy powers are shared by the President and Congress, a national policy is sometimes difficult for the United States to achieve.

A foreign policy that has the support of a majority of Members of Congress of both political parties but is opposed by the President could be considered bipartisan, but it is usually not because legislative-executive dissension can impede an effective policy as much as or more than differences between congressional members of the two parties. Such policies might be considered "bipartisan legislative-executive conflicts." An example is the congressional passage over President Reagan's veto of the Comprehensive Anti-Apartheid Act of 1986, imposing further sanctions against South Africa. Another example is the passage in October 1974 of legislation prohibiting military aid to Turkey following its Cyprus invasion.

Bipartisan foreign policy is an apt term for legislative-executive agreement, however, in a period of divided government when the President belongs to one political party and the majority of Congress belongs to the other. Since legislation and appropriations require the approval of both branches, during periods of divided government some degree of bipartisan support is essential for action.

Earlier in American history divided governments were not frequent.[2] Since the Second World War, however, the United States has had a President of one party and a congressional majority of the other party for more than half the time. (See Table 1, Presidents, Party Majorities, and Foreign Policy

Support in Congress Since 1947 at end of chapter.) Congressional majorities of the opposite party in both houses were faced by President Truman in 1947 and 1948, President Eisenhower from 1955 through 1960, Presidents Nixon and Ford from 1969 through 1976, President Reagan in 1987 and 1988, and President Bush at the beginning of his term in 1989.

In a rare situation which had not existed since the time of President Hoover, President Reagan from 1981 through 1986 faced a split Congress, with a Democratic majority in the House and a Republican majority in the Senate. In this case not only was some degree of cooperation essential between the branches, but some bipartisan cooperation was necessary between the two Chambers of Congress for the passage of legislation.

Even when the President and majority in both Houses of Congress belong to the same political party, support from minority party members may be necessary. Members of Congress often vote in temporary coalitions based on regional or other interests not related to party and minority votes are often needed to obtain a majority vote for foreign policy measures supported by the President. In addition, minority votes are usually needed to obtain the two-thirds majority required for the advice and consent of the Senate to a treaty.

Bipartisan Consensus

A bipartisan consensus may be said to exist when the President and the majority of both parties in Congress, or the Senate alone in the case of treaties, agree on a given policy. Thus a bipartisan consensus existed on such policies as containment initiated by aid to Greece and Turkey in 1947, the Marshall Plan in 1948, and the Taiwan Relations Act in 1979.

A bipartisan consensus does not necessarily mean unanimity. Policies may be supported by a bipartisan consensus and still have a substantial number of votes in opposition, as in the case of aid to Greece and Turkey in 1947.

Table 1 shows the proportion of foreign policy votes in each Congress since 1947 qualifying as a bipartisan consensus. The column, Congress Index of Bipartisanship, indicates that a bipartisan consensus existed on more than half the foreign policy votes in both Houses during seven Congresses: the 80th Congress under President Truman (1947-48), the 83rd through 86th Congresses under President Eisenhower (1953-60), the 87th Congress under President Kennedy (1961-62), and the 91st Congress under President Nixon (1969-70).[3] Since 1971 a bipartisan consensus has existed on more than half the foreign policy votes only once in the House (1971-72) and twice in the Senate (1975-76 and 1979-80). According to the index, the Senate has usually, but not always, had a higher frequency of bipartisan consensus than the House.

Bipartisan Legislative-Executive Coalitions

Often support for foreign policy does not qualify as a bipartisan consensus because it does not include a majority of both parties in both houses. Nevertheless, legislation passes because of various coalitions voting in favor.

Frequently a bipartisan coalition is formed from a majority of the President's party and enough votes from the other party that the issue is not considered partisan. An example is the Senate approval of the Panama Canal Treaties in 1978, in which 52 Democrats were joined by 16 Republicans to provide the necessary two-thirds majority.

Sometimes a "bipartisan rescue" occurs, when the majority of the President's party does not endorse one of his foreign policies, but supporting legislation passes anyway because the majority of members of the other party provide the necessary votes. An example is legislation lifting the ban on military aid to Turkey in 1978.

Other times a bipartisan "swing vote" determines the outcome of an issue. This can occur when the House or Senate are fairly evenly divided on an issue, and a relatively small group of Members representing both parties is not committed to either side. Such a group used its balance of power to determine the extent to which the future of the MX missile would be linked with arms control.[4] Similarly, the fate of aid to the Nicaraguan contras under the Reagan Administration was often determined by a group of 20-30 Members who sometimes supported aid and other times opposed it.[5]

Nonpartisan Foreign Policy

Some Members of Congress and executive officials believe the term nonpartisan instead of bipartisan should be used to make the point that partisan politics should not be a factor in foreign policy, that "politics stop at the water's edge." Chairman of the House Foreign Affairs Committee Dante Fascell wrote:

> Our objective should be renamed as a "nonpartisan" foreign policy both because our goal is broader and because it is unrealistic to see our two major parties, as amorphous as they are, united behind a foreign policy composed of hundreds of different elements. A bipartisan foreign policy implies such an unrealistic goal. What is realistic is to expect that political maneuvering to gain partisan advantage will end at our borders. This does not imply, however, that either party is not free to oppose the other when its convictions indicate that the other party's policies are bad for the nation.[6]

The concept of nonpartisanship in foreign policy appears to be a forerunner to the concept of bipartisanship. President William Howard Taft in 1912 said:

> The fundamental foreign policies of the United States should be raised high above the conflict of partisanship and wholly disassociated from differences as to domestic policy. In its foreign affairs, the United States should present to the world a united front.[7]

Among others favoring the term "nonpartisan" foreign policy were Secretary of State Cordell Hull and Senator Arthur Vandenberg. Senator Vandenberg wrote, "Bipartisan foreign policy is not the result of political coercion but of non-political conviction."[8]

On the other hand, John Foster Dulles suggested that Secretary of State Hull, or President Roosevelt's political advisers, preferred the term "nonpartisan" because they feared "bipartisan" might "concede the Republicans an equal status in a project that was now presumed to be politically profitable."[9]

National Consensus Based on Shared Assumptions

In one view, a foreign policy deserves to be called bipartisan only when it is based on a national consensus, shared assumptions, or a similar "worldview" enabling it to endure through partisan changes in administrations and Congress.[10] Accordingly, bipartisan foreign policy in the immediate post World War II period was possible primarily because the majority in both political parties and of the American people shared the belief that the Soviet Union under Stalin constituted a major threat to the free world and had to be contained by military strength.

Although both terms are ambiguous, a national consensus implies broader agreement than bipartisan consensus.[11] As an example, Senator Richard Lugar, Chairman of the Foreign Relations Committee from 1985 until 1987, spoke of finding bipartisan areas of consensus but made it clear he meant a national consensus. He said, "The foreign policy consensus that we seek is not simply one of a few dedicated Senators, but a coming together of the American people at the grass roots."[12]

Agreement in Party Platforms

Another indicator of bipartisan support for policies may be the platforms, or statement of views, adopted by each party in the quadrennial conventions to nominate candidates for President and Vice President.

Many drawbacks exist in attempting to use party platforms to determine a party's position on foreign policy. The drafting of the platform itself is a political act, done to reconcile the party's internal problems and assist the party's candidate in the election. The planks may represent the views of a faction without accurately or fully representing the view of the majority or the candidate running on them. Or, alternatively, they may be purposely vague in order to be acceptable to all factions. Some observers consider the platforms meaningless rhetoric and question the extent to which they are used.

Nevertheless, the platform does represent an effort of each party to articulate what it stands for and the position it wants to place before voters. Occasionally they indicate broad bipartisan consensus or sharp differences between the parties on particular policies.[13] One analyst notes, "While platforms contain rhetoric and self-praise, they also consist of goals and proposals that differentiate them from one another."[14]

Comparison of the 1988 party positions offers a recent example, although on individual issues analysis is difficult because the Democratic convention purposely chose to adopt a shorter platform of 4,000 words, whereas the Republicans adopted a more detailed platform of 40,000 words.[15] Nevertheless, in the 1988 platform some differences were perceptible on some foreign policies, such as Central America and South Africa.[16]

Despite notable differences, the Democratic and Republican platforms in 1988 showed several areas of agreement in foreign policy. On burdensharing, for example, the Democratic platform said that "our national strength will be enhanced by more stable defense budgets and by a commitment from our allies to assume a greater share of the costs and responsibilities required to maintain peace and liberty...." In a similar vein, the Republican platform said "although we must maintain a strong presence, the alliance has now evolved to a point where our European and Japanese allies, blessed with advanced economies and high standards of living, are capable of shouldering their fair share of our common defense burden."[17]

Policymaking Process

Those who view bipartisanship as a process look at the way a policy is made rather than the policy itself. In their view, a policy should be considered bipartisan only when representatives of both political parties have shared in making it. Senator Arthur Vandenberg wrote that to him bipartisan foreign policy meant "a mutual effort, under our indispensable two-Party system, to unite our official voice at the water's edge so that America speaks with maximum authority against those who would divide and conquer us and the free world."[18] Another observer defined bipartisanship as "the attempt to achieve unity in foreign affairs through the use of certain techniques and practices acceptable to both political parties."[19]

The chief measure of bipartisanship as a process is usually the degree and quality of consultation between representatives of the two branches and of the two parties. However, some believe the process entails more than executive-legislative consultation. They argue that the process should extend to a nationwide effort through the press and interested groups to discuss the relevant issues and arrive at a national consensus on what policy should be adopted.[20]

In summary, when people advocate a bipartisan foreign policy they may mean a policy with support ranging from simply enough votes for enactment of legislation to a national consensus based on shared assumptions, or they may mean a process of cooperation to build such support. In this paper the term encompasses both policy and process. A bipartisan foreign policy ideally means a policy that has the support of the Administration and a majority in Congress including a majority of both political parties, and that has been achieved through a process of bipartisan legislative-executive consultation.

TABLE 1. Presidents, Party Majorities,
and Foreign Policy Support in Congress Since 1947*

Year	President	Congress	Congress Index of Bipartisanship**	
			House	Senate
1947-48	**Truman (D)**	**80th (R)**	65.2	75.0
1949-50	Truman (D)	81st (D)	37.5	40.4
1951-52	Truman (D)	82nd (D)	30.4	33.3
1953-54	Eisenhower (R)	83rd (R)	60.9	61.7
1955-56	**Eisenhower (R)**	**84th (D)**	66.7	74.1
1957-58	**Eisenhower (R)**	**85th (D)**	63.3	72.0
1959-60	**Eisenhower (R)**	**86th (D)**	80.0	64.5
1961-62	Kennedy (D)	87th (D)	56.8	52.7
1963-64	Kennedy (D)	88th (D)	10.0	80.0
	Johnson (D)		28.0	58.5
1965-66	Johnson (D)	89th (D)	42.2	72.8
1967-68	Johnson (D)	90th (D)	46.3	67.0
1969-70	**Nixon (R)**	**91st (D)**	68.8	71.4
1971-72	**Nixon (R)**	**92nd (D)**	58.1	42.2
1973-74	**Nixon (R)**	**93rd (D)**	28.9	50.7
	Ford (R)		17.6	35.9
1975-76	**Ford (R)**	**94th (D)**	27.6	62.7
1977-78	Carter (D)	95th (D)	20.5	26.0
1979-80	Carter (D)	96th (D)	28.0	51.3
1981-82	**Reagan (R)**	**97th, House (D)**	47.1	
		Senate (R)		37.9
1983-84	**Reagan (R)**	**98th, House (D)**	18.9	
		Senate (R)		41.1
1985-86	**Reagan (R)**	**99th, House (D)**	14.1	
		Senate (R)		29.2
1987-88	**Reagan (R)**	**100th (D)**	27.8	42.7
1989-90	**Bush (R)**	**101st (D)**	na	na

*Bold face type indicates President and majority in Congress belonged to different political parties (D=Democrats; R=Republicans). For precise dates of presidential terms and congressional sessions: U.S. Congress. 1987-1988. Official Congressional Directory, 100th Congress. Charts: Sessions of Congress; and Presidents and Vice Presidents and the Congresses Coincident with their Terms.

**The Congress Index is the proportion of foreign policy votes on which the majority of both parties supported the President's position. McCormick, James M. and Eugene R. Wittkop, Bipartisanship, Partisanship, and Ideology in Congressional-Executive Foreign Policy Relations, 1947-1988. Journal of Politics, November 1990. Appendix supplied by authors. The McCormick-Wittkop analysis is based on roll-call votes reported in the Congressional Quarterly Almanac.

TABLE 2. Patterns of Bipartisan and Partisan Voting

Bipartisan Consensus: (President and majority of both parties in both Houses of Congress, or in Senate on treaties, agree.)

Issue	President	Senate	House
United Nations Charter August 8, 1945	Truman for	89-2	
Aid to Greece and Turkey $400 million appropriation Approved May 15, 1947	Truman for	67-23 D 34-7 R 35-16	287-108 D 160-13 R 127-94
European Recovery Program Approved April 3, 1948	Truman for	69-17 D 38-4 R 31-13	329-74 D 158-11 R 171-61
North Atlantic Treaty Approved by Senate July 21, 1949	Truman for	82-13 D 50-2 R 35-16	
Gulf of Tonkin Resolution, August 7, 1964	Johnson for	88-2 D 56-2 R 32-0	416-0 D 241-0 R 175-0
Taiwan Relations Act P.L. 96-8 Passage March 13, 1979	Carter for	90-6 D 56-1 R 34-5	345-55 D 241-14 R 34-5
ABM Treaty Approved by Senate August 3, 1972	Nixon for	88-2 D 48-1 R 40-1	

(continues)

TABLE 2. (continued)

Bipartisan Legislative-Executive Coalition: (President prevails with support of majority of President's party and sufficient votes of other party in Congress for passage.)

Issue	President	Senate	House
Senate amendment of Military Procurement Authorization (H.R. 17123) limiting to 280,000 the maximum number of troops in Vietnam after April 30, 1971, and providing for complete withdrawal of troops by December 31, 1971, rejected September 1, 1970	Nixon opposed	39-55 D 32-21 R 7-34	
Bill halting import of Rhodesian chrome to bring U.S. into compliance with U.N. sanctions against Rhodesia, passage March 14, 1977	Carter for	66-26 D 48-9 R 18-17	250-146 D 211-52 R 39-94
Panama Canal Neutrality Treaty March 16, 1978 (Two-thirds majority required)	Carter for	68-32 D 52-10 R 16-22	
Panama Canal Treaty April 18, 1978 (Two-thirds majority required)	Carter for	68-32 D 52-10 R 16-22	
Panama Canal Act of 1979 (Vote on final conference report on Panama Canal implementing legislation) P.L. 96-70 approved September 27, 1979	Carter for	63-32 D 47-9 R 16-23	232-188 D 196-70 R 36-118
Motion to table (kill) amendment to H.J. Res. 631, Continuing Appropriation, FY83, to ban use of funds after January 20, 1983, to support irregular forces in Central America, December 18, 1982	Reagan for	56-38 D 16-27 R 40-11	
Multinational Force in Lebanon Resolution (P.L. 98-119), passage September 29, 1983	Reagan for	54-46 D 2-43 R 52-3	253-156 D 123-129 R 130-27
Amendment to prohibit use of funds for deployment of U.S. armed forces participating in multinational peace force in Lebanon after March 1, 1984, rejected Nov. 2, 1983. (Amendment to H.R. 4185l, Defense Department Appropriation)	Reagan opposed		53-274 D 136-126 R 17-148
Motion to table (kill) amendment to invoke certain War Powers Resolution time limits for U.S. military operations in Persian Gulf, September 18, 1987	Reagan for	50-41 D 15-34 R 35-7	

(continues)

TABLE 2. (continued)

Bipartisan Swing Vote: (Approximately equal number of Members on each side of issue, with outcome determined by uncommitted bipartisan group)

Issue	President	Senate	House
Adoption of concurrent resolution to permit use of funds appropriated in FY83 to develop a basing method for the MX missile and to conduct MX test flight, Senate May 25 and House May 24, 1983	Reagan for	59-39 D 12-33 R 47-6	239-186 D 91-168 R 148-18
Adoption of amendment to authorize production of 15 MX missiles but prohibit the obligation of funds unless Congress approves by joint resolution after April 1, 1985; May 31, 1984	Reagan opposed		199-196 D 182-54 R 17-142
Motion to table (kill) amendment to produce no additional MX missiles in FY85 but keep production line open pending study of new mobile Midgetman missile, June 14, 1984	Reagan for	48-48 D 5-38 R 43-10 (V.P. broke tie by voting for)	
Adoption of joint resolution authorizing $1.5 billion to procure 21 MX missiles in FY85, March 19 and 26, 1985	Reagan for	55-45 D 10-37 R 45-8	
H.J. Res. 444 to approve President's request of $36.25 million for continued military and non-military aid to the Nicaraguan contras; House rejected February 3, 1988; Senate supported February 4, 1988.	Reagan for	51-48 D 12-41 R 39-7	211-219 D 47-207 R 164-12
Amendment to substitute Democratic plan to provide $30.8 million for humanitarian aid to contras for Republican plan (H.J. Res. 484); House approved March 3, 1988.	Reagan opposed		215-210 D 212-37 R 3-173
Passage of Democratic plan to provide $30.8 million for humanitarian aid to contras (H.J. Res. 484); House rejected March 3, 1988.	Reagan opposed		208-216 D 203-45 R 5-171

(continues)

TABLE 2. (continued)

Bipartisan Rescue: (President's position wins without support of own party's majority but with support of majority of other party)

Issue	President	Senate	House
Amendment permitting end to ban on aid to Turkey, Senate and House passage July 26 and August 1, 1978	Carter for	57-42 D 30-32 R 27-10	208-205 D 130-141 R 78-64

Bipartisan Legislative-Executive Conflict: (Presidential position fails with opposition of majority of both parties in Congress)

Issue	President	Senate	House
Amendment to Defense Appropriations bill prohibiting introduction of U.S. ground combat troops into Laos and Thailand, December 15, 1969	"In line with expressed intention of President"	73-17 D 35-15 R 38-2	Voice vote
Second 1973 Supplemental Appropriation, containing ban on Cambodia bombing Passed House May 10, 1973; Senate May 31, 1973	Vetoed by President Nixon	284-96 D 201-16 R 83-80	73-5 D 46-1 R 27-4
Passage of continuing appropriation with prohibition against military aid to Turkey until progress on military forces on Cyprus, October 17, 1974	Ford opposed	Voice vote	191-33 D124-22 R 67-11
Override of veto on sanctions against South Africa, September 29, 1986	Reagan opposed	78-21 D 47-0 R 31-21	313-83 D 232-4 R 81-79

(continues)

TABLE 2. (continued)

Partisan Legislative-Executive Conflict: (Presidential position fails but has support of majority of his party in at least one house of Congress)

Issue	President	Senate	House
War Powers Resolution (P.L 93-148), passed over veto November 9, 1973	Nixon opposed	75-18 D 50-3 R 25-15	284-135 D 198-32 R 86-103
Amendment to Intelligence Authorization Act, FY 1983, to halt covert aid to Nicaraguan contras; passed House July 28, 1983 (not acted on in Senate)	Reagan opposed		228-195 D 210-50 R 18-145
Motion to kill amendment to S.J.Res. 159 requiring the President to submit a report under section 4(a)(1) of War Powers Resolution that the multinational force in Lebanon became involved in hostilities August 29, 1983; agreed to September 29, 1983	Reagan for	55-45 R 55-0 D 0-45	
Motion to kill amendment to FY 1988 Dire Emergency Supplemental bill H.R. 5026) to provide $27.14 million in humanitarian aid and release $16 million in stockpiled military aid to Nicaraguan contras; Senate rejected August 10, 1988.	Reagan opposed	57-39 D 51-2 R 6-37	
Amendment to FY 1989 Defense Appropriations (P.L.100-463) to provide $27.14 million in humanitarian aid to Nicaraguan contras and to establish procedures for congressional release of $16 million in stockpiled military aid to Nicaraguan contras; Senate adopted August 10, 1988; accepted by House September 23, 1988.	Reagan opposed but signed	49-47 D 49-4 R 0-43	

Recorded votes have been compiled primarily from Congressional Quarterly Almanac, Vol. I, 1945 through Vol. XLIV, 100th Congress, 2nd Session, 1988. Washington, Congressional Quarterly, Inc., 1989.

3

Postwar Record of Bipartisanship

The concept of a bipartisan foreign policy has taken shape and become controversial primarily since World War II, the period to which this study is limited.

Early Postwar Bipartisan Foreign Policy Model: Building Consensus

At the end of World War II, a bipartisan foreign policy process evolved in part from a deliberate effort to move away from the policy of isolationism which had widespread support before the war. Many Americans perceived that the war and the development of technology affecting transportation, communications, and weapons had brought about a dramatically altered international situation that made isolationism obsolete.

In just a few years, a consultative process helped shape several policies that became the core of U.S. foreign policy. These included establishment of the United Nations and other international organizations, the Marshall Plan, and major components of the policy of containment of Soviet communism such as aid to Greece and Turkey and the North Atlantic Treaty.

Postwar Planning and the United Nations

The modern genesis of a bipartisan foreign policy came during the war in connection with postwar planning. Many remembered the defeat of the Treaty of Versailles after the first

World War, which was widely attributed to President Wilson's failure to win Republican support for the League of Nations. Representatives of both branches took initiatives during the war to prevent a recurrence.

Early in 1942 Chairman of the Senate Foreign Relations Committee Tom Connally asked Secretary Hull, who had been a Senator from 1931 until 1933, to send State Department representatives on a regular basis to assure that the entire committee, "not only the Democrats," were informed.[21] Subsequently the Secretary often met with the committee. The meetings were considered helpful, although later Senator Connally expressed the view that President Roosevelt should have invited some congressional leaders to attend the wartime international conferences because Secretary Hull's briefings on the conferences were limited to what the President had told him.[22]

Also in 1942 President Roosevelt created the Advisory Committee on Post-War Foreign Policy and included in the membership several Members of Congress of both political parties. The first congressional members were Senator Connally and Senator Warren R. Austin, a minority member of the Foreign Relations Committee designated after consultations with Republican leaders. Later members included Senators Walter F. George and Elbert D. Thomas, and Representatives Sol Bloom and Luther A. Johnson, Democrats, and Senator Wallace A. White and Representatives Charles Eaton and Richard Welch, Republicans.[23]

As the war progressed and postwar planning picked up momentum, bipartisan consultation increased. In 1944, prior to the Dumbarton Oaks Conference, Secretary Hull requested the Senate Foreign Relations Committee to appoint eight Members, four Democrats and four Republicans, to confer with him on the draft plan for an international security organization. The Committee appointed Senators Connally, Alben Barkley, George, and Guy Gillette, Democrats, and Vandenberg, White, and Austin, Republicans, and Robert La Follette, Progressive.

During this period the State Department also frequently consulted with a bipartisan group of Senators known as the B2H2 group, consisting of Senators Joseph Ball and Harold

Burton (Republicans) and Lister Hill and Carl Hatch (Democrats).

As the election of 1944 approached, in August Secretary of State Hull said, in response to questions at a press conference, that he would welcome a conference with Governor Thomas E. Dewey, the Republican candidate for President, to discuss a nonpartisan approach to postwar organization. Governor Dewey accepted this proposal and appointed John Foster Dulles, his adviser on foreign affairs, to confer with Secretary Hull. After that conference, Mr. Dulles was kept informed of the progress made at Dumbarton Oaks.

When the United Nations Conference met to draft the Charter in San Francisco in June 1945, the U.S. delegation included several Republicans: Senator Vandenberg, Representative Eaton, Commander Harold Stassen, and John Foster Dulles as senior adviser.

The effort succeeded in winning the necessary support for the new organization. The Senate gave its advice and consent to the United Nations Charter on July 28, 1945, by a vote of 89-2.[24] The implementing legislation, the United Nations Participation Act (P.L. 79-264), was also passed by large margins (65-7 in the Senate on December 4, 1945, and 344-72 in the House on December 18, 1945).

Aid to Greece and Turkey: Containment

In 1947 and 1948 the control of Congress shifted to the Republicans, Senator Vandenberg consolidated his position of foreign policy leadership, and the core of the postwar bipartisan foreign policy of containing the Soviet Union within its existing sphere was formulated.

An immediate foreign policy crisis arose when the United Kingdom informed the United States on February 24, 1947, that it would cease aid to Greece and Turkey on April 1, 1947. President Truman invited members of the foreign policy committees to discuss the crisis on February 27 and he met with another bipartisan congressional group for the same purpose on March 10.[25] On March 12 he gave the speech enunciating what came to be known as the Truman Doctrine, to "support free peoples who are resisting attempted subjugation by armed minorities or by outside pressures."

Republican leaders apparently did not believe the consultation had been adequate. Nevertheless, Senator Vandenberg rallied support for the program.[26] In May the Senate passed the Greek-Turkish Aid Program by a vote of 67 to 23 and the House by a vote of 287 to 108, with a majority of both parties in both houses voting in favor. President Truman appointed Republican Dwight P. Griswold, former Governor of Nebraska, to be head of the American aid mission to Greece.

The Marshall Plan

More thorough bipartisan consultation accompanied the establishment of the Marshall Plan or European Recovery Program. Although the plan apparently was initiated in the executive branch without congressional consultation, after June 5, 1947, when Secretary of State Marshall proposed a long-range economic assistance program, both branches worked together in developing the program later enacted.

Both branches established study groups that were bipartisan or nonpartisan in nature. On July 29, 1947, the House of Representatives created a Select Committee on Foreign Aid headed by Christian Herter to visit Europe and conduct an independent study of the situation. A special joint subcommittee of the House Armed Forces and Appropriations Committees under Everett Dirksen also investigated conditions abroad. Senator Vandenberg as Chairman of the Senate Foreign Relations Committee commissioned a study by the Brookings Institution of the administration of the foreign aid program. Partly in response to a suggestion of Senator Vandenberg the President created a Committee on Foreign Aid comprised of private citizens and chaired by Averell Harriman.

On September 29, 1947, President Truman held a bipartisan meeting to discuss the results of the conference of European nations who wished to participate and the study groups that had been established by the President.[27] He proposed an emergency appropriation to deal with immediate needs in Europe to be followed by enactment of a long-range program the next year. Shortly afterwards he called a special session of Congress which adopted the interim aid program, the Foreign Aid Act of 1947. The interim aid program to deal with immediate needs permitted more time for study and discussion of the longer range recovery program.

The Senate Foreign Relations and House Foreign Affairs Committees held lengthy hearings and made modifications in the program presented by the Administration. Both Houses adopted the European Recovery Program by large majorities, 69 to 17 in the Senate and 329 to 74 in the House.

Some have noted the consultation process for the Marshall Plan was not perfect, suggesting, for example, that the Administration should have consulted Senator Vandenberg and Representative Eaton, chairmen of the foreign policy committees, in drafting the Administration's proposed legislation.[28] Nevertheless, the bipartisan and interbranch study process was exemplary in many respects, and the Marshall Plan has been widely acclaimed as an effective U.S. foreign policy.

North Atlantic Treaty

The North Atlantic Treaty is also widely considered an excellent example of bipartisan foreign policy. One of the first major steps toward it took place in the Republican-controlled 80th Congress when Senator Vandenberg pursued with Under-Secretary of State Robert Lovett the question of military association between the United States and Europe. Together they developed the Vandenberg Resolution in favor of "progressive development of regional and other collective arrangements for individual and collective self-defense" in accordance with the U.N. Charter.[29]

Subsequently President Truman authorized the Secretary of State to enter exploratory conversations with representatives of European countries, and in April 1949, twelve nations signed the North Atlantic Treaty. On June 6 the Foreign Relations Committee, now chaired by Senator Connally since the

Democrats had regained a majority, reported the treaty favorably. The report commended the treaty as exemplary of how an important foreign policy issue should be handled:

> First the committee and the Department of State considered together the problems facing the United States in this field and the courses of action best suited to deal with them. The Senate then gave the President its advice as to particular objectives to be sought. The executive branch faithfully followed the advice of the Senate and, during the negotiations with the other governments, consulted fully with the committee, which played an effective part in formulating the terms of the treaty. From the beginning the deliberations of both the committee and the Senate on Senate Resolution 239 and the treaty have been conducted on a wholly nonpartisan basis. Finally, in order to give the American and other peoples the earliest possible opportunity to consider the treaty, its terms were made public considerably in advance of signature, as soon as they had been agreed upon by the negotiating governments.[30]

The Senate approved the treaty on July 21, 1949, by a vote of 82 to 13.

The above policy areas in which a bipartisan consensus was developed in the early postwar period--support for the United Nations, containment, foreign assistance--remained essentially bipartisan, supported through administrations and Congresses of differing political compositions. In April 1989 the North Atlantic Treaty Organization celebrated its 40th anniversary, testifying to its durability. A number of other actions, such as the passage of the Taiwan Relations Act in 1979, have had bipartisan support in recent decades, but few have been called bipartisan foreign policies or achieved the prolonged consensus attained by the original bipartisan foreign policies.

Areas Lacking Consensus

The golden era of bipartisan foreign policy did not last long and it did not cover all areas of foreign policy at the time. Although the Vietnam War has come to symbolize the breakdown of consensus on foreign policy, many believe the breakdown began with the Korean War in 1950 or even earlier on

U.S. policy toward China in the late 1940s. Some contend there was never a bipartisan foreign policy in some areas, particularly Asia.

Troops to Europe

Even on some aspects of policies considered bipartisan considerable dissension had sometimes appeared. Most noteworthy of these is the issue of troops to Europe. President Truman announced on September 9, 1950, that the number of U.S. forces stationed in Western Europe would be substantially increased. Senator Robert Taft, a prominent Republican, opposed the move and Senator Wherry, the Republican floor leader, introduced a resolution opposing the assignment of ground forces in Europe pending the formulation of policy on the matter by Congress.

A "Great Debate" ensued and significant differences were revealed on both defense strategy and the respective powers of the President and Congress to dispatch force. On April 4, 1951, the Senate adopted a greatly modified resolution by a bipartisan consensus of 69-21 (D 42-2; R 27-19). S. Res. 99 expressed the sense that the threat to security required stationing U.S. troops abroad for the joint defense effort, but also that the dispatch of additional divisions should be subject to congressional approval and that the major portion of troops should be supplied by the NATO partners.

China in the Late 1940s

After the surrender of Japan in September 1945, the civil war in China between the Communists and Nationalists resumed. U.S. attempts in the following period to promote a coalition government and prevent a Communist takeover failed. After an unsuccessful effort by General Marshall to mediate between the rival groups, Nationalist China collapsed militarily and the Nationalist government of Chiang Kai-shek fled to Taiwan.

Apparently little legislative-executive consultation occurred on China. Senator Vandenberg acknowledged bipartisan efforts in other areas, but said that he had not been consulted in respect to China policy, only handed State Department pronouncements.[31]

On the other hand, other observers contend that while a bipartisan consultative procedure on China did not develop, until the fall of Nationalist China U.S. decisions had the support of Members in both parties. In particular, the Republican 80th Congress passed the China aid program of 1948.[32] The program was not as carefully planned as the European Recovery Program had been, and was partly an Administration attempt to win support of the "China Lobby" in Congress. Congress altered the program by reducing the economic aid while adding military assistance.[33]

After the Communist victory on the Chinese mainland in 1949, disagreement over China policy continued for many years and foreshadowed continuing division of opinion on U.S. policy toward countries facing civil war involving national Communist parties.

One of the main reasons China policy came to be considered partisan was that the question of "who lost China" became an issue in the 1952 Presidential election. One observer wrote that Republican candidate Dwight Eisenhower

> unequivocally charged the Democrats with the "loss" of China to the Communists. [Democratic candidate Adlai] Stevenson countered by defending the Administration's record and by pointing out America's limited ability to affect the outcome of the Chinese civil war.[34]

Republican Senator Joseph McCarthy exacerbated the divisions when he alleged Communist elements in the State Department were responsible.

Korean War

When North Korea invaded South Korea on June 25, 1950, President Truman proposed a U.N. Security Council resolution calling on U.N. members to help South Korea, and ordered U.S.

military assistance to the South Koreans prior to consultations with Congress. On June 27, 1950, he met with 14 congressional leaders. The next day Senator Taft, who had not been included in the consultations, criticized the method of providing U.S. assistance. He claimed that the Administration's Far East policies were an invitation to attack because Korea had not been included in a description of the U.S. defense perimeter. He said the general principle of the policy was right and he saw no choice except to back the policy and provide every necessary resource to the U.S. troops, but he also complained that the President had brought about U.S. intervention in the war without consulting Congress. He said "there has been no pretense of any bipartisan foreign policy about this action."[35]

In turn, many Democrats blamed the Republicans for the decline in bipartisan foreign policymaking. Senator Tom Connally wrote:

> However, it was the Korean fighting, so essential to the world's future security and peace, that brought a wide-open foreign-policy split between Democrats and Republicans. As the fighting developed the Republicans, instead of closing ranks, sought to cast grave doubts about the necessity for Truman's action. This was pure politics because privately many of these same legislators supported the fighting in Korea. But mothers and fathers of American boys in Korea were led to believe by this Republican sniping that the war was improper and unjust. So naturally many of them became bitter against the administration.[36]

Deep division of opinion having partisan aspects was evident again after April 11, 1951, when President Truman relieved General Douglas MacArthur of his command in the Far East after policy differences on the conduct of the war. Senator Wherry introduced a resolution praising General MacArthur, and the Senate Armed Services and Foreign Relations Committees subsequently held joint hearings on his dismissal and on U.S. policy in the Far East. The committees decided against issuing a report on grounds that a unanimous report was not possible and a majority report followed by a minority report would exacerbate differences and add confusion.[37]

Vietnam

Policy toward Vietnam does not stand out clearly as either partisan or bipartisan; it varied over the decade-long military involvement. Nevertheless, Vietnam is often considered a watershed in legislative-executive relations that marked a reassertion of congressional power in foreign policy.

On the one hand Vietnam policy might be considered bipartisan because it developed and endured through both Democratic and Republican Presidencies. Key elements such as necessary appropriations were supported by bipartisan votes in Congress.

Both the House Foreign Affairs Committees and Senate Foreign Relations Committees endorsed the idea of a Pacific pact prior to the negotiation of the Southeast Asia Collective Defense Treaty. The latter treaty was signed on September 8, 1954, by Secretary of State John Foster Dulles, Republican Senator H. Alexander Smith, and Democratic Senator Mike Mansfield. On February 1, 1955, the Senate approved the treaty by a vote of 82 to 1.[38]

A decade later, in 1964, both Houses adopted by overwhelming majorities the Gulf of Tonkin Resolution sought by Democratic President Lyndon Johnson. In the Senate the vote was 88 to 2; the House supported it by a unanimous vote of 416 to 0.[39] The Administration used the resolution as a congressional authorization for a substantial increase in U.S. combat forces in Vietnam.

On the other hand, opinion on Vietnam divided during the 1960s and the war became an issue in the Presidential elections of 1964 and 1968. In the 1964 election, Republican Presidential candidate Senator Barry Goldwater called for stronger military action in Vietnam. President Johnson was elected as a moderate on the war in comparison with Goldwater, and the politics of the situation helped account for the overwhelming passage of the Gulf of Tonkin Resolution, with neither party wanting to look "soft" on communism.[40]

After July 18, 1965, when President Johnson announced a large increase in the number of U.S. forces in Vietnam, dissent about the war began to grow in the society and in Congress and was an important factor in President Johnson's decision not to seek reelection in 1968. President Nixon undertook to reduce U.S. ground troops and increasingly rely on South Vietnamese forces, while negotiating a cease fire that was concluded in January 1973.

During the Nixon Administration Congress began to use its power of the purse to ensure that the President carried out his stated intentions not to expand involvement into neighboring countries. One of the first such measures was an amendment to the Defense Appropriations bill prohibiting U.S. ground combat participation in Laos and Thailand.[41] The House adopted the measure on December 8, 1969, by voice vote; the Senate adopted it on December 15 by a vote of 73-17 with a majority of both parties in favor.

The U.S. incursion into Cambodia in 1970 to attack North Vietnamese sanctuaries crystallized opposition and distrust in the Senate. Although President Nixon gave assurances that all U.S. forces had been withdrawn, the Senate passed the Church-Cooper amendment to the foreign military sales bill prohibiting the use of funds to maintain American combat troops in Cambodia, but the measure was deadlocked in conference and ultimately not included in that legislation. The essence, namely that "in line with the expressed intention of the President" none of the funds "authorized or appropriated pursuant to this or any other act" could be used to introduce ground combat troops into Cambodia, was incorporated in the Supplemental Foreign Assistance Authorization Act, P.L. 91-652. The House passed this measure on December 9, 1970, by a vote of 249-102, and the Senate on December 16 by a vote of 72-22, with a majority in both parties in support.

Similarly, the U.S. bombing of Cambodia in the spring of 1973, after U.S. forces had been withdrawn from Vietnam in March, crystallized opposition in the House and brought about a bipartisan consensus in Congress to further restrict U.S. action. On May 10, 1973, the House passed an appropriations bill banning further bombing of Cambodia by a vote of 284-96 The Senate passed a stronger measure on May 31, 1973 by a vote of 73-5. President Nixon vetoed the measure on June 27 and the House failed to override, but the President agreed to compromise legislation setting August 15 as the cutoff date for use of funds to "support directly or indirectly combat activities in or over Cambodia, Laos, North Vietnam and South Vietnam or from off the shores of" those nations.[42] Although he signed the measure, President Nixon wrote the leaders of both Houses expressing his "grave personal reservations" about the consequences.

The Cambodian bombing also boosted legislation seeking a permanent curb on the President's use of armed forces without a declaration of war or other authorization by Congress. This effort culminated in the passage of the War Powers Resolution over President Nixon's veto. The House passed its version, H.J. Res. 542, on July 18, 1973, by a vote of 244 to 170 (D 172-61; R 72-109). The Senate passed a different version, S 440, on July 20 by a vote of 72-18 (D 50-4; R 22-14). When President Nixon vetoed the conference compromise on October 24, 1973, each House overrode the veto. As in the vote on the original version, a bipartisan consensus existed in the Senate, but the majority of Republicans in the House voted to sustain the President's veto.[43]

Multinational Force in Lebanon

Complaints about lack of bipartisanship in legislative-executive cooperation were also raised after the withdrawal of Marines from Lebanon in 1984.

In 1982 President Reagan sent U.S. Marines to participate in a multinational force assisting the Lebanese government to restore its authority and maintain order. After two Marines were killed by artillery fire on August 29, 1983, and casualties mounted, legislative-executive and partisan differences also grew and many in Congress sought a more active role in determining how long the forces should remain.

Although President Reagan submitted reports to Congress under the War Powers Resolution, he did not cite section 4(a)(1) of the Resolution that would trigger the requirement that forces be withdrawn within 60 to 90 days unless authorized by Congress to remain. Some Members sought to invoke this provision. The President and Speaker of the House Thomas O'Neill agreed on compromise legislation, the Multinational Force in Lebanon Resolution, which determined that the provision of Section 4(a)(1) had become operative on August 29, 1983, and also authorized the Marines to remain for 18 months.[44] The measure represented a bipartisan coalition but not consensus; it was opposed by a majority of Democrats in both Houses, but had the support of enough Democrats in the House to secure passage.[45] In the Senate, where the Republicans had a majority, an amendment by Democratic Majority Leader Robert Byrd requiring the President to submit a report under the War Powers Resolution or withdraw the forces by the end of the year was stopped by a straight party vote of 55 Republicans to 45 Democrats.

Scarcely had the Multinational Force in Lebanon Resolution been passed than on October 23, 1983, a suicide truck-bomb attack killed 241 Marines, bringing about a rethinking in Congress and the nation of the mission of the U.S. forces. Representative Clarence Long introduced an amendment to the Defense Appropriation bill to cut off funding for the force after March 1, 1984. The amendment was defeated on November 2, 1983, by a 153-274 vote that was a bipartisan coalition (D 136-126; R 17-148) but not consensus since a majority of Democrats voted for the amendment.

When Congress reconvened in January 1984, a number of bills were introduced offering various policy options, such as immediate withdrawal of the Marines, reducing the 18 month authorization to a shorter period, redeploying the Marines to ships, and replacing the multinational force with a U.N. peacekeeping force.[46] Debate began to fall along more partisan lines. In the House, after a draft resolution prepared by the Democratic Caucus received considerable attention, Republican Members took issue with what they considered a partisan tone and a bypassing of normal procedures. The issue became moot, however, when President Reagan announced the redeployment of U.S. Marines offshore on February 7, 1984.

After the withdrawal of Marines from Lebanon, President Reagan called for a restoration of bipartisanship, which he criticized Congress for "undermining" by "second-guessing" his decision to keep the troops in Lebanon.[47] Senate Majority Leader Robert Byrd countered:

> The American participation failed because the assumption upon which our policy was grounded proved unworkable. Neither the leadership of President Gemayel nor the viability of the Lebanese Armed Forces was up to the task of building a strong leading coalition in Lebanon.... The fractured political and military conflict which has engulfed Lebanon did not occur because the U.S. Congress debated policy there.[48]

South Africa

Deep differences of opinion on solutions to the problems of southern Africa have long beset U.S. policy. By the end of the Reagan Administration, many analysts considered South Africa a policy area that lacked bipartisanship.

In 1985 partisan divisions were apparent on the issue of whether to impose economic sanctions to South Africa. On June 5, 1985, the House passed a bill imposing economic sanctions against South Africa by a vote of 295-127 (D 239-6; R 56-121). The majority of Republicans joined with President Reagan in opposing the measure. The Senate passed a milder version by a bipartisan consensus of 80-12 (D 44-0; R 36-12) on July 11, 1985. Some Republican Senators threatened a filibuster on the conference report. During the delay, President Reagan on September 9, 1985, imposed some sanctions by Executive order.

In 1986, however, Congress developed a bipartisan consensus strong enough to override a Presidential veto. The House passed a bill calling for stronger sanctions against South Africa by voice vote and the Senate passed a sanctions bill by a vote of 84-14 (D 47-0, R 37-14). President Reagan vetoed the bill, but the House overrode the veto of President Reagan by a vote of 313-83 (D 232-4; R 81-79), the Senate by a vote of 78-21; (D 47-0; R 31-21). Thus the Comprehensive Anti-Apartheid Act (P.L. 99-440) went into effect on October 2, 1986, with the majority of both parties in both the Republican Senate and the Democratic House voting to override President Reagan's veto.

Nicaragua and Central America, 1981-88

Policy on Central America also frequently lacked bipartisan support during the Reagan Administration. After 1979, when the Sandinista government overthrew the Somoza regime in Nicaragua, deep differences of opinion developed on how much of a threat the Marxist regime posed, and what action the United States should take to prevent the possible spread of communism.

Both branches were concerned with some actions of the Sandinista government and its growing ties with Cuba. But as reports appeared of covert U.S. actions to destabilize the Sandinista regime, an increasing number of Members of Congress, particularly in the Democratic House, voiced opposition to the Reagan Administration's policy.

Nicaraguan policy came to exemplify a partisan legislative-executive impasse, where neither the policy sought by the Administration nor the policy sought by the congressional majority could receive full-hearted support. Although bipartisan coalitions often supported the President's position, they frequently imposed checks and restraints that the President opposed.

The result of yearly legislative-executive battles and, from 1981 through 1986, compromises between the Republican Senate and Democratic House, was a policy perceived as having many inconsistencies and ambiguities. In 1982 the House rejected an amendment by Rep. Tom Harkin to prohibit the use of CIA or Defense Department funds to assist anti-Sandinista groups and approved by a 411-0 vote a less restrictive amendment by Rep. Edward Boland favored by the Administration to prohibit the use of funds for overthrowing the Government of Nicaragua.[49] In 1983 the House twice voted to cut off funds to the contras, but the Senate approved the funds; the conference agreement provided funds but set a limit on the amount that could be spent for paramilitary activities and also directed the President to seek peace negotiations.[50]

In 1984 the Senate agreed to the House rejection of supplemental funds for the contras and barred expenditure of additional appropriated funds unless approved by a joint resolution. Key elements in the Senate position were suspicions that the earlier Boland amendment had been violated and the Administration's failure to inform the Intelligence Committees of the mining of Nicaraguan harbors.[51] In 1985 the Senate voted for but the House voted against the release of the previous year's funding; Congress approved $27 million for aid to the contras in fiscal year 1986 but restricted it to non-lethal, humanitarian purposes. In 1986 Congress appropriated $100 million for aid to the contras and included military as well as humanitarian assistance.[52]

In 1987 legislative-executive tension intensified because the Republicans no longer had a majority in the Senate to assist the Administration's position. In addition, the 1987 investigation of the Iran-contra affair revealed that, from October 1984 through 1985 when assistance to the contras had been prohibited by law, President Reagan had directed the National Security Adviser to secure funds for assistance from private and third country sources, thus circumventing the intention of Congress.[53] Accomplishing the same end were funds diverted from the sale of weapons to Iran. These actions resulted in the prosecution of principals in the activity and some convictions. Although President Reagan wanted to continue military aid for the contras, a majority in Congress refused and pressed harder for a negotiated settlement.

The impasse brought new efforts for a peaceful solution. In July 1987 the Administration invited Speaker of the House Jim Wright to participate in developing a peace plan and negotiated solution for the conflict in Nicaragua. A bipartisan Wright-Reagan plan was developed which served as a catalyst for a plan developed by the Central Americans themselves. Although dissension soon recurred on elements of the new peace plan and on the Speaker's active role in negotiations, Congress voted in both 1987 and 1988 to supply some further humanitarian assistance to the contras, but again with extensive controls and restraints.[54]

Fresh Effort at Bipartisan Foreign Policy

At the end of the 1980s, a number of factors produced a favorable environment for a fresh effort to construct a bipartisan foreign policy. It had become clear to many that bitter legislative-executive disputes over Central America, South Africa, and other policy areas were impeding effective policy making. New international realities such as the changing relative economic power of the United States were becoming impossible to ignore. The advent of Gorbachev's "new thinking" in the Soviet Union challenged the assumptions on which the postwar policy of containment had been built.

New calls for a bipartisan foreign policy came from many sides. Former Secretaries of State Henry Kissinger and Cyrus Vance wrote of "our deep belief that the security of free peoples and the growth of freedom both demand a restoration of bipartisan consensus in American foreign policy" and suggested bipartisan objectives.[55]

In taking office, President Bush pledged the restoration of a bipartisan foreign policy. He said in his inaugural address, "A new breeze is blowing, and the old bipartisanship must be made new again." Similarly, Secretary of State James Baker spoke strongly of the need for bipartisanship in hearings on his nomination.[56]

A congressional initiative to rebuild a bipartisan foreign policy appeared fruitful. Senators David L. Boren and John C. Danforth, a Democrat and Republican respectively, wrote in December 1987: "Since we arrived in the Senate about a decade ago, partisanship within the institution has increased alarmingly," and called for efforts to "provide the starting point for a new spirit of bipartisanship. What is needed is both a general statement of foreign policy principles in the manner of the Vandenberg Resolution and an ongoing process for working out specific differences as they arise, but before they are ripe for legislative action."[57] In 1988 they and four other Senators wrote both Presidential candidates asking that the future President hold regular monthly meetings with congressional leaders.

President Bush began to hold such meetings on February 9, 1989, and by the end of October 1989 five meetings had been held, and participants described them as productive. Four were routine meetings and one was called on July 31 to discuss policy in the aftermath of the release of videotapes showing the killing of U.S. Marine Lt. Col. William R. Higgins by a radical faction in Lebanon. Members invited have been the Majority and Minority Leaders of the Senate, the Speaker and Minority Leader of the House, and the Chairmen and Ranking Members of the Foreign Relations and Foreign Affairs, Intelligence, and Armed Services Committees. From the executive branch, the meetings have been attended by the President, Vice President, Secretary of State, Secretary of Defense, and National Security Adviser.

In addition, Secretary of State Baker undertook other meetings with bipartisan congressional groups on specific policies such as Central America and South Africa, discussed below.

Not all evidence pointed toward commitment to a bipartisan foreign policy, however. Some policy areas, such as dealing with General Noriega in Panama or responding to the foreign policy initiatives of President Gorbachev, did not appear to be included in the bipartisan efforts, at least for the time being. In addition, in several instances the Bush Administration challenged anew various congressional actions as unconstitutional and infringing on Presidential responsibilities in foreign affairs.[58] Moreover, some observers contended both the President and Secretary of State were primarily concerned with domestic political advantage, not foreign policy needs.[59]

Bipartisan Agreement on Central America

The first major action toward a bipartisan foreign policy was a surprise agreement concerning Central America, one of the areas over which partisan conflict had been most pronounced during the Reagan Administration. On March 24, 1989, President Bush announced: "We signed today in the Cabinet

Room a bipartisan accord on Central America which sets out the broad outlines of U.S. policy toward the region."[60]

Signing the agreement on the congressional side were Speaker of the House James C. Wright, Jr., Senate Majority Leader George Mitchell, House Majority Leader Thomas S. Foley, Senate Republican Leader Robert Dole, and House Republican Leader Robert Michel.

The agreement provided for continued humanitarian aid to the contras in the next year while a new peace accord signed by the five Central American Presidents at Tesoro Beach, El Salvador, on February 14, 1989, took effect. That accord provided for voluntary demobilization, repatriation or relocation of the contras, and democratic reforms leading to elections in Nicaragua on February 25, 1990.

The legislative-executive agreement also addressed the process of bipartisan consultation. It said:

> We also endorse an open, consultative process with bipartisanship as the watchword for the development and success of a unified policy toward Central America. The Congress recognizes the need for consistency and continuity in policy and the responsibility of the Executive to administer and carry out that policy, the programs based upon it, and to conduct American diplomacy in the region. The Executive will consult regularly and report to the Congress on progress in meeting the goals of the peace and democratization process, including the use of assistance as outlined in this Accord.
>
> ...The United States need not spell out in advance the nature or type of action that would be undertaken in response to threats to U.S. national security interests. Rather it should be sufficient to simply make clear that such threats will be met by any appropriate Constitutional means. The spirit of trust, bipartisanship, and common purpose expressed in this accord between the Executive and the Congress shall continue to be the foundation for its full implementation and the achievement of democracy, security, and peace in Central America.[61]

In addition, as part of the compromise, Secretary of State Baker sent a letter to congressional leaders, promising that none of the funds for humanitarian assistance would be spent after November 1989 unless the President received letters of approval from the bipartisan leadership of Congress and relevant House and Senate authorization committees (House Foreign Affairs and Senate Foreign Relations) and Appropriations subcommittees.⁶² Some Members raised questions as to whether this constituted a legislative veto, which the Supreme Court declared unconstitutional in *INS* v. *Chadha*; but others considered it an informal method which has been used on several occasions since the *Chadha* decision.⁶³

In less than a month, legislation implementing the agreement was complete. Both the Senate and the House passed the measure on April 13 by majority votes in both parties.⁶⁴ On April 19, 1989, President Bush signed the measure into law, P.L. 101-14. The legislation authorized up to $49.75 million humanitarian assistance to the contras through February 28, 1990, plus $4.166 million for medical assistance to civilian victims and $5 million to the Agency for International Development for administration.

The agreement was a compromise. Many considered it a way to end the contra war while providing opportunities for Congress to halt the assistance if it was not satisfied with the Administration's observance of the conditions. Others emphasized it provided for a rethinking of the issue if the Sandinistas did not abide by their commitment to hold a free election in February 1990. One observer wrote, "Although its supporters claim to have achieved a bipartisan consensus on Central America, the fact is that both sides have only agreed upon a procedure, not a consensus policy."⁶⁵ In any event, the procedural arrangements provided a basis for finding policy agreement.

Movement on South Africa

The Bush Administration also began to consult with Congress in the hopes of developing a bipartisan policy toward South Africa, an area on which the two branches had differed in policy approaches during the Reagan Administration. In particular, Congress had enacted sanctions against South Africa over a Presidential veto in 1986. Secretary Baker said the Administration was engaged in a dialogue "to see if we can come forward with an agreed course so the United States can speak with one voice and might be able to have some impact on what happens in South Africa, because we're having scant impact right now."⁶⁶

In addition to meetings between Secretary Baker and congressional leaders, Assistant Secretary for African Affairs Herman J. Cohen met with Sen. Paul Simon and Rep. Howard Wolpe, chairmen of the African affairs subcommittees of the Foreign Relations and Foreign Affairs Committees, and Sen. Edward Kennedy, chief sponsor of a comprehensive sanctions bill. Rep. Wolpe took the lead in organizing a bipartisan group of 26 Members, including 15 Democrats and 11 Republicans, to negotiate on a compromise U.S. policy on South Africa and draw up legislative plans.⁶⁷

According to press accounts, the Administration was seeking an understanding that would provide time for the Administration to test its approach with the South African government and persuade it to negotiate with a wider range of South African leaders. The objective would be legislative-executive agreement on a package of measures, intended to promote negotiations, which would include greater flexibility for the President to ease sanctions in response to positive steps by the South African government.⁶⁸ Senator David Boren said that prior to congressional adoption of a new legislative framework with more Presidential flexibility, it would be necessary for the Administration to signal a change from the Reagan Administration's negative view of sanctions and acknowledge they have been helpful in bringing change.⁶⁹

The election on September 6 of a new South African government headed by F. W. De Klerk, who had pledged to make changes in the apartheid policies, added a new factor to the situation. Although on October 2, 1989, the Administration reported in response to a congressional requirement that the South African government had taken no fundamental steps to dismantle apartheid, it asked Congress to give the new government a reasonable time to demonstrate its intentions before adding new sanctions.⁷⁰ Congressional advocates of new sanctions appeared satisfied with this approach for the time being, especially as the new government took some steps toward negotiations including the release of Nelson Mandela on February 11, 1990.

4

Perspectives on Bipartisan Foreign Policy

Proponents and opponents of a bipartisan foreign policy generally agree on the strengths and weaknesses of such a policy, but they give different weights to them.

Bipartisanship for Strength and Continuity

Proponents emphasize that a bipartisan policy has support from both branches of government and therefore is stronger and less confusing to other nations. Senator David Boren, Chairman of the Senate Select Committee on Intelligence, wrote, "Divisiveness, the United States has learned, emboldens its enemies to test its resolve and confuses and demoralizes its friends and allies around the world."[71]

Proponents also contend that support from both parties ensures that a policy survives changes resulting from elections. Senator Charles Percy, Chairman of the Foreign Relations Committee from 1981 until 1985, wrote: "unity, support, or consistency is unlikely without a greater measure of bipartisanship."[72]

Secretary of State Baker said after the Central American agreement: "I think if you examine American foreign policy throughout the postwar era, one truth certainly shines through. From President Truman's support for NATO to President Reagan's I.N.F. agreement, every important achievement has enjoyed sustained bipartisan support."[73]

Cautions on Bipartisanship:
Need for Criticism and Accountability

Opponents emphasize the necessity of critical debate on a policy and the danger that a bipartisan policy may stifle criticism for a variety of reasons. Members of Congress may be reluctant to question a course of action when they have participated in the planning. Support for a policy may seem so widespread that some Members who oppose it may be reluctant to speak out against it. Pleas for unity may make criticism seem uncooperative or unpatriotic.

Senator Robert Taft raised this issue during the Vandenberg era of bipartisanship. He said on January 5, 1951:

> As I see it, Members of Congress, and particularly Members of the Senate, have a constitutional obligation to reexamine constantly and discuss the foreign policy of the United States. If we permit appeals to unity to bring an end to that criticism, we endanger not only the constitutional liberties of the country, but even its future existence.
>
> Certainly when policies have been determined, unity in execution is highly desirable, and in the preparation for and the conduct of war it is essential.... But it is part of our American system that basic elements of foreign policy shall be openly debated.... Whatever the value of unity, it is also true that unity carried to unreasonable extremes can destroy a country...the best safeguard against fatal error lies in continuous criticism and discussion to bring out the truth and develop the best program.[74]

More recently other observers have complained that the postwar bipartisan consensus prevented serious debate of foreign policy actions, such as the augmentation of forces in Vietnam, and development of new policies to meet changing world circumstances. One writer contended, "If opposition is not mounted by the party out of power, then it does not enter into the formal political process."[75] In this view political figures who challenged the established policy, either from the right or the left, were discredited:

> Henry Wallace, Barry Goldwater, Eugene McCarthy, Fred Harris, George McGovern, George Wallace and Jerry Brown have lost "credibility", that is, political relevance, because they stood for views or constituencies that challenged the prevailing foreign policy consensus.

Each story, of course, is different, but the pattern confirms the assertion that it is politically costly, if not suicidal, to swim against the bipartisan current.[76]

The writings of this same analyst illustrate, however, that perspective is shaped by agreement or disagreement with the substance of a bipartisan foreign policy. In his view, it "was not bipartisanship as such, but a particular type of bipartisanship that was essentially conflict-oriented and expansionist, that led to failure" because the postwar bipartisan consensus was "premised on a dominance that no longer exists but which the United States continues to pursue by relying to an ever greater extent on the military instruments of diplomacy."[77]

Need for Accountability and Party Responsibility

A second criticism is that bipartisanship can cloud party responsibility for a foreign policy and make it difficult for the electorate to hold either party or any particular candidate accountable. When a foreign policy is clearly the responsibility of the President and his party in Congress, ideally citizens can oppose the policy by voting against candidates of the party responsible. But when a policy is held to be bipartisan, citizens cannot vote against it because there is no party clearly in opposition to it.

Not all analysts find accountability and bipartisanship incompatible. A House Republican Policy Committee study of bipartisan foreign policy contended that the breakdown of the bipartisan consensus led to greater congressional power and independence in foreign affairs, and that the institutional characteristics of the legislative branch have "created a political disconnect separating the exercise of congressional power in foreign affairs from accountability for the effect of those actions."[78] It concluded that a higher level of congressional power in foreign affairs requires a much greater accountability of Members of Congress.

In addition, the degree of accountability for any specific foreign policy even without bipartisanship may be questioned. Presidents and Members of Congress are elected for many and diverse reasons and foreign policy stands are only one factor in voting. Because U.S. elections are not plebiscites on specific policies, even when a President has a majority in Congress, he may not have party agreement on any specific policy stand.

Bipartisanship When Helpful

Finally, many policy analysts agree that bipartisan foreign policy has a mixed record. It is not the panacea of its most ardent advocates but may be useful at some times in some areas. One observer concluded:

> The bipartisan approach to foreign relations has neither met the expectations of its most dedicated adherents nor justified the strident cries of its severest critics. It has not fulfilled the hopes of its strongest advocates because partisan discord has prevailed toward several important problems in American foreign affairs.... The bipartisan principle has not borne out the dire predictions of its most passionate foes because it has unquestionably made possible forceful demonstrations of national unity in the face of grave and recurrent external crises.[79]

Secretary of State John Foster Dulles wrote:

> Because bipartisanship in foreign policy thus cuts across our basic constitutional and traditional political views, it ought to be used only sparingly and when the needs and perils are so great that exceptional measures are demanded."[80]

Put another way, Presidents turn to bipartisanship when they need more support for a policy. Senator Sam Nunn said: "...when their ox is in the ditch, they'll turn bipartisan to get a hand in hauling it out."[81]

5

Issues

Four key issues underlie the differing perspectives on a bipartisan foreign policy. What are the appropriate roles for Congress and the President in making foreign policy? Are there fundamental differences between the two parties on foreign policy? Should foreign policy be treated differently from domestic policy? Can and should party politics be kept out of foreign policy?

Roles of President and Congress in Foreign Policy

A basic issue concerns the respective roles of the President and Congress in foreign policy. The Constitution divides the foreign policy powers between the President and Congress in a manner that has been described as "an invitation to struggle for the privilege of directing American foreign policy."[82] To illustrate, Congress has the power to raise revenue, make appropriations and laws, and regulate commerce with foreign nations; the President is the chief executive and carries out the laws. Congress has the power to declare war and raise and maintain the armed forces; the President is Commander in Chief. The President makes treaties and appoints Ambassadors and other public Ministers "by and with the advice and consent of the Senate." As a result, dominance in foreign policy has shifted between the two branches from time to time throughout U.S. history according to events in the United States and the world and personalities in the executive branch and Congress.

Bipartisanship in foreign policy is based on the premise that cooperation between the President and Congress in foreign policy is essential, but the meaning of cooperation varies.

Those who believe that the President has a special, superior role in foreign policy may view a bipartisan foreign policy as a method to obtain the support of Congress for the President's policy. John Foster Dulles when Secretary of State expressed this view: "Under the Constitution, the President, and the President alone, decides on how to conduct foreign affairs. He can conduct them alone or with others, as he desires; the decision is his.... Bipartisanship can come about only through Presidential invitation."[83]

When President Reagan called for a return to bipartisanship in April 1984, after the withdrawal of the Marines from Lebanon, he left the impression he meant Congress should help build support for policy. He said:

> Presidents must recognize Congress as a more significant partner in foreign policy-making, and, as we have tried to do, seek new means to reach bipartisan executive-legislative consensus. But legislators must realize that they, too, are partners. They have a responsibility to go beyond mere criticism to consensus-building that will produce positive, practical and effective action.[84]

Those who believe Congress shares the responsibility for formulating foreign policy may view a bipartisan foreign policy as a method for developing a partnership between the President and Congress, in which Congress participates in shaping a foreign policy from its inception. Senator Vandenberg referred to the necessity for consultation from the beginning, saying, "I don't care to be in on the crash-landing unless I can be in on the take-off."[85]

Opposition to bipartisanship is based on the premise that under the separation of powers system the President makes foreign policy and the appropriate role for Congress in foreign policy is adversarial. This position allows the executive branch the flexibility it wants. Congressional supporters of the adversarial position reject the idea of becoming a partner of the executive branch on the grounds that they might lose their freedom to criticize. They believe Congress has adequate influence on foreign policy decisions from the risk of Senate defeat of a completed treaty, or congressional refusal to pass legislation or appropriate funds to implement a policy.

"Micromanagement"

During the Reagan Administration the term "micromanagement" came into vogue to imply that Congress is too involved in details or playing an excessive role in the conduct of foreign policy. Then Vice President Bush complained that "In the last twenty years we've witnessed a departure from the way in which this nation has conducted its foreign policy for nearly two centuries. Congress has asserted an increasingly influential role in the day-to-day micromanagement of foreign policy and even of foreign operations."[86]

Discussion of micromanagement has increased during the Bush Administration and President Bush cited it as a factor in his veto of legislation concerning coproduction of the FS-X aircraft with Japan.[87]

Recently the term was linked with the concept of bipartisan foreign policy when six Senators wrote both Presidential candidates in 1988 stating their hope "that in return for more real consultation by the executive branch, Congress would agree to accept less congressional intervention and micromanagement of foreign policy."[88]

Congress has generally agreed that the President as head of the executive branch has responsibility for the carrying out of foreign policy and the day to day conduct of foreign relations. But concerns arise over how effectively the President and other executive branch officials guide this conduct. In addition, there is no clear line where setting direction of or making foreign policy ends and the conduct or implementation of foreign policy begins.

As Congress has become more active in foreign policy, the quantity of legislation relating to foreign policy has increased and with it the number of legislative restrictions. In recent years Congress has frequently given detailed directives and imposed numerous restrictions and reporting requirements in the foreign assistance program and other legislation relating to foreign policy. As one measure, the number of reporting requirements in foreign affairs legislation increased from 200 in 1973 to more than 700 in 1988.[89] From the congressional point of view, directives and restrictions were a method of shaping policy, and reporting requirements were necessary to obtain information and assure that the executive branch followed congressional intent.

Although the term "micromanagement" is new and legislative provisions have increased, complaints against legislative interference or restrictions by Congress are not new or restricted to Presidents of a single political party. In 1978, the Carter Administration distributed a list entitled "Restrictions on Presidential authority to provide assistance to foreign nations and conduct foreign operations," and Senator George McGovern said:

> If the idea can be generated that Congress is meddlesome and an impediment to effective Presidential action, some administration officials may feel Congress might be rendered more docile in the future.[90]

Source of Differences on Foreign Policy

Another basic issue is whether any fundamental differences on foreign policy exist between the two major political parties. Do foreign policy disputes follow partisan lines or result from other factors? If disputes result from other factors, efforts to promote bipartisan cooperation might need to be directed instead at reconciling these factors.

Both political parties sometimes imply that each party has a distinct foreign policy or that important foreign policy differences exist between the parties. The 1988 Democratic Platform, for example, said, "We believe that we must reassume a role of responsible active international leadership based upon our commitment to democracy, human rights and a more secure world...." The 1988 Republican Platform said, "The old Democrat world view of realistic anti-communism, with real freedom as its goal, has been abandoned by today's national Democrat

Party.... Today's Republican foreign policy has been tested and validated. Our formula for success is based on a realistic assessment of the world as it is, not as some would like it to be."

In addition, on many occasions party affiliation and loyalty seem to be a factor in the votes of Members of Congress on foreign policy. Studies of votes on foreign aid issues have found Members more likely to support a President of their own party.[91]

Nevertheless, many believe that other factors discussed below are more influential than party affiliation and account for the fact that some members or factions of a party may have foreign policy views sometimes closer to those of the majority in the other party.

Ideological Differences

Many analysts believe that foreign policy views are shaped by central value systems or basic philosophies that are shared by some members of both parties. These value systems have been called a variety of names including the "tough-minded" vs. the "tender-minded," "conservative" vs. "liberal," "idealist" vs. "realist," "isolationist" vs. "internationalist," "extrovert" vs. "introvert," and the "security culture" vs. the "equity culture."[92] One analyst who surveyed public opinion concluded that "when compared to the more traditional yardsticks of opinion analysis, party identification and political views, the national idealist and national self-interested classification scheme proved to be a better indicator of opinion on issues of foreign policy."[93]

Similarly, some analysts have found that ideological divisions dominate relations on foreign policy between the Congress and the President, and that ideology provides the continuity in foreign policy voting patterns. After analyzing foreign policy votes in Congress they reported:

> Liberals, conservatives, and moderates within both parties tended to vote similarly on foreign policy issues, regardless of the President in power. While party ties enhanced the level of support for the President, ideology clearly was more important in virtually all of the analyses. In this respect, we may have been looking in the wrong place

to find foreign policy consistency. Instead of focusing on bipartisanship, we might be better advised to focus on the ideology of congressional members.[94]

Institutional Differences

Finally, some differences on foreign policy arise from the separate institutional interests of the executive and legislative branches. Institutional differences are usually over the process of formulating policy. The executive branch prefers to keep a free hand in foreign policy, while Congress seeks restraints to assure itself a voice. But differences on the process are often intertwined with issues of substance.

At a minimum, perennial differences between the two branches occur over foreign policy issues involving the war power and the treaty power.

A persistent issue has been whether the President's power as Commander-in-Chief permitted him to send troops into potential hostilities abroad in a particular instance or whether the constitutional power of Congress to declare war required that any such action be authorized by Congress. Congress attempted to clarify the issue by the passage of the War Powers Resolution (P.L. 93-148) over the veto of President Nixon in 1973. Nevertheless, legislative-executive differences over the policy of using U.S. forces and whether the process required authorization from Congress recurred in such instances as the increase of military advisers in El Salvador in 1981, the multinational force in Lebanon and the landing in Grenada in 1983, the bombing of Libya in 1986, the naval escort of reflagged Kuwaiti vessels in the Persian Gulf in 1987, the invasion of Panama in 1989, and the dispatch of forces to Saudi Arabia in 1990.

Differences of opinion over the treaty power have occurred time and again over the President's use of executive agreements to undertake important commitments and the President's reinterpretation or termination of a treaty. Issues concerning the treaty power were intermingled with issues concerning the merits of the policies in debate on approval of the Panama Canal treaties of 1978 to relinquish control of the canal to Panama, the termination of the mutual defense treaty with Taiwan in 1979, and the reinterpretation of the ABM treaty in 1986.

Disagreements on such institutional questions may sometimes appear partisan because Members of Congress of a President's own party are more likely to support him. Republican Senators Robert Taft and John Bricker were champions of congressional war and treaty powers during the Democratic Administration of President Truman. Because during most of the 1980s there has been a Republican President and a Democratic Congress, in the past decade Republican Members of Congress have frequently been the spokesmen for executive power and Democratic Members have defended congressional war and treaty powers.

Uniqueness of Foreign Policy

Another issue is whether foreign policy should be made or treated any differently from other policies. Is there any reason to seek bipartisanship in foreign policy more than in domestic policy?

On the one hand, it might be contended that no matter what the issue, a policy is stronger if it has the support of both branches and both parties, and good policy is made in essentially the same way. In this view, some of the attributes of a bipartisan foreign policy process, such as obtaining a variety of perspectives in advance, consulting with people who will be required to support the policy, and encouraging full debate, are simply common sense measures that should be applied in making any policy.

On the other hand, some believe that foreign policy has a unique need for unity and continuity because of the involvement of other countries. When executive officials and legislators are espousing different policies, other nations may be confused or believe that U.S. policy is weak and could be easily changed because opinion is divided. Or a foreign government may be reluctant to rely on a U.S. commitment if it believes the commitment is apt to be overturned by the next election.

Still others argue that foreign policy decisions can make the difference between war and peace and, therefore, bipartisan support is more essential than it is for other policies.

The Partisan Context:
Can Foreign Policy Be Separated from Politics?

A final issue is whether bipartisanship can exist in foreign policy when partisanship is intense in other areas. Can and should "politics stop at the water's edge?"

To some extent it appears impossible to keep domestic politics out of foreign policy. Political parties are a basic part of the U.S. governmental system. The President is the leader of a political party as well as of the United States. He usually appoints persons of the same party to head the Department of State and other agencies conducting foreign affairs and expects them to advance the aims of both the party and the nation. Each party searches for issues and methods to promote its own interests and diminish the election prospects of the other party.[95]

Both political parties have large permanent offices and each party has policy and study committees in Congress that consider foreign policy as well as domestic issues. For instance, in 1984 Frank Gregorsky from the Republican Study Committee prepared a paper entitled, "What's the Matter with Democratic Foreign Policy?" criticizing the views and actions of many Democrats in Congress.[96] In 1987, the Chairman of the House Democratic Study Group and more than a hundred other Democratic Members of Congress commenced a law suit against the Reagan Administration in an attempt to trigger the time limit of the War Powers Resolution in the Persian Gulf situation.[97]

At the same time, somewhat ironically, the American party system itself may serve as a brake on partisanship in foreign policy. The two parties are decentralized and their leadership is diffused at the local, State, and national level. Even in each House of Congress party leaders have limited power over their members. Each party encompasses a wide range of voters who do not always vote according to party affiliation. The differences in ideology and on issues between the two parties are not always clear, and it is uncertain which issues are decisive in the minds of voters.

Little party responsibility exists in the sense that Members are held accountable for their party's performance or feel obligated to vote according to the party's platform or instructions. Instead, Members of Congress retain a certain independence in their vote, and it is difficult for party leaders to maintain party discipline. In foreign policy the independence may be greater than in domestic matters; one observer contends, "Clearly, on foreign policy issues, party cohesion is less likely than on other issues to be a factor in the decisions of Members of Congress."[98]

Despite calls for a renewed bipartisan foreign policy, the Bush Administration began in what appeared to be an intensely partisan atmosphere. On March 9, 1989, the Senate rejected the nomination of former Republican Senator John Tower to be Secretary of Defense by a vote of 53 (52 Democrats and 1 Republican) to 47 (44 Republicans and 3 Democrats). On June 6, 1989, the Speaker of the House, Democrat Jim Wright, ended his tenure after vigorous pursuit of ethics questions by Republican whip Newt Gingrich. Many saw little hope for a bipartisan foreign policy, but others contended bipartisanship would develop in policy areas of urgency and immediacy since without such an approach effective action might not be possible.

6

Building a Bipartisan Foreign Policy

The history of postwar foreign policy indicates that if policymakers want to develop a bipartisan foreign policy, several methods for doing so have proved useful.

Techniques of a Bipartisan Foreign Policy

Consultation

Consultation between the branches and including members of both political parties is probably the most widely advocated method of establishing a bipartisan foreign policy.[99] In addition to the important role personalities play, four determinants of effective consultation have been identified:[100]

(1) The range of Members of Congress consulted needs to portray enough views and concerns to design a policy that receives the necessary support. While the President can speak authoritatively for the executive branch, Congress has no similar single spokesman. The leadership, relevant committees and subcommittees, and individual Members with particular concerns offer varying perspectives and valuable insights on issues, but consultation with a representative group may be adequate.

(2) The timing of consultation must be early enough to affect policy. From a congressional point of view, consultation is not meaningful if it occurs after a decision has been made or when there is no room for modification of a policy.

(3) The issues selected for consultation should be significant. Consultation needs to occur on all policies involving a major commitment of armed forces or funds or sustained national support. Foreign policy embarrassments abroad could be reduced by consultation on all treaties and nominations or any issue requiring legislation or appropriations.

(4) The attitudes of both branches should be receptive to consultation. At best both the President and Congress would enter consultations in a cooperative spirit, but at least each branch could acknowledge the legitimate role of the other and try to understand its problems.[101]

Regarding consultation between the two political parties, one observer has described the requirements of complete bipartisanship thus:

> (1) Collaborators of the opposition party would have to be delegated by their own party, not merely selected by executive authorities....
> (2) They would have to be consulted on all major foreign policy problems, to be defined by joint agreement....
> (3) Consultation would have to take place before any final decision was reached by a politically responsible official of the administration....
> (4) On those subjects where agreement was reached by consultation, the leaders of both parties would also collaborate in the use of all currently available devices of party discipline to rally their respective party cohorts behind the policy decisions....[102]

For some time various Members of Congress have suggested institutionalizing consultation by such means as establishment of a permanent consultative group consisting of Administration officials and congressional leaders.[103]

Appointments

In the past a frequent method of promoting bipartisanship was through appointments of members of the opposing party to high executive positions. In 1940 President Roosevelt appointed Republicans Henry Stimson, who had been Secretary of State under President Hoover, as Secretary of War and Frank Knox, who had been the Republican candidate for Vice President in 1936, as Secretary of the Navy. President Truman appointed

John Foster Dulles, who had been a foreign policy adviser to the Republican candidate for President, Governor Thomas Dewey, as one of the delegates to the first session of the United Nations General Assembly; Warren Austin, a Republican, as U.S. Representative to the United Nations; and John Sherman Cooper, a Republican, as alternate delegate to the U.N. General Assembly and Consultant to the Secretary of State on North Atlantic Council matters. Mr. Dulles also accompanied Secretaries of State James Byrnes, George Marshall, and Dean Acheson as a Republican adviser at meetings of the Council of Foreign Ministers established by the United States, the United Kingdom, and the Soviet Union to discuss postwar peace treaties.

In at least one case, such appointments have become institutionalized. Each year the President appoints two members of Congress, alternating between the Senate and House but always including one Democrat and one Republican, to the U.S. delegation to the U.N. General Assembly.

To count as bipartisan, foreign policy appointees need to be trusted and representative members of the other party rather than nominal members. Some observers did not herald the appointment of Jeane Kirkpatrick as U.S. representative to the United Nations, as a move toward a bipartisan foreign policy, although she was a Democrat at the time President Reagan appointed her, because her views were not representative of prevailing Democratic leaders, and later she officially switched to the Republican Party.

In a similar vein, the appointment of non-partisan careerists from the Foreign Service or similar institutions to Ambassadorships or other important foreign policy positions may decrease partisanship in policymaking.

Bipartisan Commissions

Bipartisan commissions have been established on several occasions by either the President or Congress to deal with divisive foreign policy issues. While such commissions have had varying degrees of success in their missions, they have provided a channel of legislative-executive communication by including Members of Congress as members or advisers or by working closely with Congress.

In 1983 President Reagan appointed the Commission on Strategic Forces, a bipartisan group of eleven members headed by former (and present) National Security Adviser Brent Scowcroft, to review the land-based intercontinental ballistic missile system and alternative basing systems for the MX missile. The Scowcroft Commission recommended deploying 100 MX missiles in existing Minuteman silos and developing a new, smaller mobile missile, Midgetman. Several key Members of Congress who had worked with the Commission made clear that their support for the MX missile depended on acceptance of certain of its recommendations by the Administration, and the commission was found useful by many Members of Congress and the Administration.[104] But one observer contended that the report was a divided document that failed to present a clear, coherent strategy and that made it inevitable that the differing political forces would "eventually go their separate ways."[105]

Urged by bipartisan House and Senate resolutions, President Reagan in 1983 also appointed a National Bipartisan Commission on Central America, headed by former Secretary of State Henry Kissinger, to advise on long-term policy toward Central America. The Commission recommended a program of emergency economic and military assistance and a long term program of development assistance. In 1984 the Administration submitted legislation based on the commission's recommendations. Congress appropriated close to the level of funds recommended but it did not enact most of the programs recommended and included various restrictions.[106] Central American policy remained a contentious issue.

President Reagan appointed a third bipartisan commission in 1983, the Commission on Security and Economic Assistance, to conduct a review of the foreign assistance programs and find ways to generate additional public support. The Commission, chaired by Frank Carlucci, recommended higher levels of funding, support of economic policy reforms, a new agency, and greater flexibility in administering development aid. The Carlucci Commission did not receive much publicity, but the outcome was much the same as that of the Kissinger Commission; five years later the same problems remained and the House Foreign Affairs Committee set up a bipartisan Task Force to consider essentially the same problems.[107]

Some contend that bipartisan commissions have not been successful and are used to avoid responsibility for making decisions.[108] Occasionally it is not even possible for a bipartisan commission to get off the ground. In 1986 Congress provided for a bipartisan monitoring commission to report on progress in negotiations for a Central American peace plan and reform of the Nicaraguan contras. Each party was to appoint two members of the commission, and the four commissioners were to agree on a fifth member who would be chairman. The next year Democratic and Republican leaders appointed the four commissioners, but the four members were unable to agree on a chairman and the commission was dissolved.[109]

Somewhat unique because of its composition, oversight function, and long life is the Commission on Security and Cooperation in Europe. Congress established the Commission in 1976 to monitor the implementation of the 1975 Final Act on Security and Cooperation in Europe of the Helsinki Conference.[110] The Commission membership consists of 9 Senators and 9 Representatives (five from the majority party and 4 from the minority party), with 3 members of the executive branch representing the Departments of State, Defense, and Commerce. The executive branch opposed the establishment of the Commission as an intrusion into the negotiating and implementation responsibilities of the executive branch. Nevertheless, the two branches have worked together through it as the Conference on Security and Cooperation in Europe mechanism progressed in resolving East-West problems. In one view the two branches have provided a balance, with Members of Congress emphasizing human rights and the executive branch emphasizing the arms control issues, and their cooperation in the Commission has strengthened the U.S. negotiating position.[111]

Bipartisan Congressional Observer Groups

Even before the defeat of the Treaty of Versailles in 1919 and 1920, Presidents sometimes appointed Senators or Representatives to help negotiate treaties in order to enhance the prospects of Senate approval of the agreement and passage of any necessary implementing legislation.

Among the earliest, President Madison appointed Senator James A. Bayard and Speaker of the House Henry Clay to help negotiate the Treaty of Ghent following the War of 1812, and both resigned their congressional seats to do so. President McKinley appointed three Senators including one Democrat to negotiate the treaty with Spain following the Spanish-American war. Even President Wilson appointed a former diplomat who was a Republican, Henry White, to accompany him to negotiate the Versailles Treaty. President Harding appointed Henry Cabot Lodge and Oscar Underwood, the Chairman and Ranking Member of the Senate Foreign Relations Committee to represent the United States at the Washington Naval Conference.[112]

More recently the practice, except for the U.S. delegation to the United Nations General Assembly described above, has been for Members of Congress to serve as advisors or observers rather than delegates or negotiators. As one example, Republican Senator Frank Carlson and Democratic Senator Gale McGee served as congressional advisers to the Conference on Antarctica in 1959. Some conferences, such as the U.N. 3d Law of the Sea Conference in the 1970s and early 1980s, the U.N. World Food Conference in 1974, and the Geneva Meeting on Refugees and Displaced Persons in Southeast Asia in 1979, have had a dozen or more congressional advisers.

The initiative for congressional observers sometimes comes from Congress. The House and Senate appointed bipartisan congressional observer groups, with members from each political party, for the 1985 and 1986 talks on strategic arms control at Geneva. The idea was proposed by Majority Leader Robert Byrd, a Democrat, approved by Senate resolution, and accepted by the Republican Reagan Administration. In 1989 the Senate passed S. Res. 105 reconstituting and reauthorizing the Senate Arms Control Observer Group of 20 Members.[113] The House has also appointed arms control observer groups for several years. On June 15, 1989, the Speaker and Minority Leader each appointed 11 Members as observers to the strategic arms reduction talks and two Members to the chemical weapons talks.

Congressional groups have also been appointed to observe other events affecting U.S. foreign policy. In 1986 President Reagan appointed an observer group for the Philippines' election that included four Senators and Representatives, two from each political party. In 1987 the Senate established a Central American Negotiations Observer Group for any bilateral or multilateral negotiations dealing with the question of peace in Central America. The group was reestablished in 1989.[114]

Bipartisan Congressional Efforts

All congressional committees are bipartisan in structure, with ratios reflecting the overall composition of Congress and Members assigned by the party caucuses. While on straight party votes the majority would win, voting is frequently not along party lines. On occasion, congressional panels may be created to foster bipartisanship. In the Senate, for instance, the Select Committee on Intelligence has an 8-7 majority-minority ratio and its Vice Chairman, who replaces the Chairman when he is absent, is from the minority party.

Committees also sometimes undertake special efforts to be bipartisan or nonpartisan. A recent example would be the Task Force on Foreign Assistance established by the House Foreign Affairs Committee to review the foreign aid program. Chairman Dante Fascell and Ranking Minority Member William Broomfield organized the task force, appointing Representatives Lee Hamilton and Benjamin Gilman as co-chairmen, and all members of the committee were invited to participate.

The task force initiated close consultation with the Administration and sought to deal with the Administration's concern over legislative restrictions as well as congressional concerns. It reported that "foreign assistance is vital to promoting U.S. foreign policy and domestic interests, but that the program is hamstrung by too many conflicting objectives, legislative conditions, earmarks, and bureaucratic red tape."[116] At the same time, the task force sought to maintain accountability by proposing methods for more rigorous congressional oversight and closer legislative-executive consultation. The report made numerous recommendations for significant changes in the foreign assistance program.

The resultant bill, H.R. 2655, authorized foreign assistance of $11.6 billion for each of the two fiscal years 1990 and 1991 and substantially rewrote the foreign aid legislation. It was passed by the House on June 29, 1989, by a bipartisan vote of 314-101 (D 197-46; R 117-55). The measure was not enacted during the 101st Congress, however, because it was not acted upon by the Senate, which had not participated in the task force.

Thus, for congressional efforts, it is necessary for consultation and cooperation to be bicameral as well as bipartisan. Some bicameral cooperation at the end of congressional consideration of an issue is assured by conference procedures on bills passed with significant differences between the House and Senate version. Consultation between the two chambers at an earlier stage often depends on informal personal contact between Members and staff.

A noteworthy example of an effort by the two chambers to work together from the outset was the joint hearing and report on the Iran-contra affair. The majority report was agreed to by all the Democratic members of the committee and three out of five Republican Senators but no Republican Representatives.[116]

Staffing Patterns

Staffing patterns of executive branch agencies and congressional committees also affect bipartisanship. Two major approaches are available for congressional committee staffing.

One is to have an integrated, essentially nonpartisan staff available both to majority and minority members. The Legislative Reorganization Act of 1946 authorized each standing committee of the House or Senate to appoint four professional staff members in addition to clerical staff on a permanent basis "without regard to political affiliations and solely on the basis of fitness to perform the duties of the office", to be assigned to the chairman and ranking minority member as the committee deemed advisable.[117] While the act permitted assignment of personnel to the minority, the Foreign Relations Committee, for example, had a professional, nonpartisan staff for many years hired by a subcommittee composed of the two ranking majority and minority members.[118]

The other approach is to have staff designated specifically to serve the majority and minority parties. The Legislative Reorganization Act of 1970 increased the number of professional staff members to six and provided that when a majority of the minority members of a committee requested, two such professional staff members could be selected by majority vote of the minority.[119] In January 1979 the minority members of the Senate Foreign Relations Committee elected to have a minority staff, and since that time that committee has had a majority and minority staff.[120] The number of staff with partisan ties also increased after Senate Resolution 60, approved June 12, 1975, permitted individual Senators to have a personal staff member participate in the work of committees.[121]

Some observers believe that a nonpartisan professional staff promotes bipartisanship by minimizing partisan political considerations. On the other hand, Senator Robert Dole, in proposing minority staff for the Commission on Security and Cooperation in Europe in 1980, contended, "Before something can be bipartisan, ...it must be composed of two different parties. Therefore, in order for the Commission staff to be bipartisan, it first must have people chosen by the minority as well as the majority members. A staff selected entirely by the Democratic Chairman and Democratic Staff Director is not a bipartisan staff."[122]

The executive branch has both nonpartisan and partisan staff. Civil service employees and Foreign Service Officers serve the incumbent President without regard to party affiliation. Heads of agencies who make decisions, however, are appointed by the Administration in power.

Sharing Credit and Blame

Another method of promoting a bipartisan foreign policy is for political leaders of one party to share credit for successes with the other party, and for both parties to share in the political liability for unpopular actions. An example of credit sharing that has been cited was the Truman Administration's willingness to acknowledge the contributions of Senator Arthur Vandenberg.[123] Examples of sharing political liability were the support of Senators Robert Byrd and Howard Baker for the Panama Canal Treaty, and the shielding of legislators from industry representatives by President Carter's special trade representative Robert Strauss in negotiating the Trade Act of 1974.[124]

Attitudinal Requirements

If an Administration or Congress wants to develop a bipartisan foreign policy, techniques and methods alone are not enough. More fundamental are certain attitudes including reciprocal trust and understanding, a willingness to cooperate and compromise, and mutual restraint in actions and rhetoric.

Reciprocal Trust and Understanding

One of the most important attitudes necessary is trust between the two branches. Senator Pell, Chairman of the Foreign Relations Committee, expressed a frequently heard congressional view:

> What leads to a breakdown of bipartisanship stems at least in part, often entirely, from a lack of openness and frankness by the Executive in the consultation process.
> ...There are serious disagreements about...issues--but those disagreements are nothing compared with the sense of betrayal that results from being misled or misinformed. This is what drains the reservoir of good will and leads to the breakdown of the consultation process itself.[125]

Mutual recognition and understanding of each other's roles and problems are also essential. Cooperation is more difficult if executive branch officials denigrate the legitimate role of Congress in foreign policy, or Members of Congress fail to recognize legitimate needs of the Administration for carrying out foreign policy effectively.

Some analysts link trust and understanding. They believe that the necessary trust can be built by attempts to understand the problems and viewpoints of the other branch, as well as by scrupulous adherence to laws and mutual commitments.

Willingness to Compromise

Another attitudinal requirement is a willingness to accept advice and views from the other side and sometimes to incorporate them into policy by compromising or finding an option acceptable to all. Senate Robert Taft said in 1951 that a bipartisan foreign policy was:

> a proper ideal and the minority will always be ready to answer any appeal for advice and cooperation. Only there cannot be a bipartisan foreign policy unless it is a policy on which both parties agree, and it is unlikely that there can be such agreement unless the Administration is more inclined to give consideration to the views of the minority and to modify its own views than it has done in recent months. We certainly would be prepared to make concessions, but certainly the policy of concessions should not be a one-way street.[126]

Without a willingness to compromise, often the other mechanisms for devising a bipartisan policy fail. Senator Dole told the story of how President Wilson had invited members of the Foreign Relations and Foreign Affairs Committees to dinner to discuss the proposed League of Nations. Two key Republican Senators, William E. Borah and Albert B. Fall, refused to attend because they did not wish to be bound to silence. But when the treaty came before the Senate, neither President Wilson nor the chief opponents would compromise, and the treaty failed. In the words of Senator Dole, "The dinner at the White House had been a fine gesture, but only a gesture, and it failed to achieve its ultimate objective."[127]

Mutual Restraint in Actions and Rhetoric

A third requirement is some restraint in partisan rhetoric and action. While the stifling of criticism stands as one of the great dangers of bipartisanship, excessively partisan criticism may undo any efforts to consult and build a consensus.

Some have suggested an important element in a bipartisan foreign policy is to refrain from making a foreign policy issue a test of party loyalty. Senator Arthur Vandenberg said:

> I have relied upon the validity of my actions to command whatever support they may deserve. I have never made any semblance of a partisan demand for support and I never shall. ...I expect every Republican, like every Democrat, to respond to his own conscience. I expect them all to act not as partisans but as Americans. I expect none of them to yield their judgments, at such an hour, to the political dictates of any party managers.[128]

An admonition from President Washington's farewell address seems appropriate:

> There is an opinion that parties in free countries are useful checks upon the administration of the government, and serve to keep alive the spirit of liberty. This within certain limits is probably true, and in governments of a monarchial cast, patriotism may look with indulgence, if not with favor, upon the spirit of party. But in those of the popular character, in governments purely elective, it is a spirit not to be encouraged. From their natural tendency, it is certain there will always be enough of that spirit for every salutary purpose. And there being constant danger of excess, the effort ought to be, by force of public opinion, to mitigate and assuage it. A fire not to be quenched, it demands a uniform vigilance to prevent it bursting into a flame, lest instead of warming, it should consume.[129]

7

Conclusion

In one view, a bipartisan foreign policy in the immediate post-World War II period was possible only because of shared assumptions based on unique conditions, and it is unrealistic to expect that these conditions will be duplicated. The shared assumptions came from the common experience of World War II, in which failure to stop the aggression of Adolf Hitler led to eventual world war, and Stalin's Soviet Union expanded to dominate Eastern Europe. A mutually perceived threat encouraged foreign policy unity within the United States and an abundance of resources facilitated U.S. leadership. As the threat changed and diminished and U.S. relative economic power declined, in this view, the underlying agreement necessary for a bipartisan foreign policy evaporated.

Nevertheless, many calls are being made for a new attempt at a bipartisan foreign policy. Such calls are often made when the legislative and executive branches are presided over by different parties, for some degree of bipartisan cooperation is essential for an effective foreign policy in a period of divided government.

Moreover, a bipartisan foreign policy has proved useful in the past in several circumstances: (1) during a national crisis, such as World War II, when a clear threat to the nation rendered a united effort essential; (2) when new approaches were needed to overcome divisiveness, as in the case of Central America in the late 1980s; and (3) when major changes in foreign policy direction appeared necessary to meet new world conditions, as at the end of the Second World War when the United States moved from a position of isolationism to world leadership. The latter circumstance became apparent again when the policies of Soviet President Gorbachev revolutionized the politics and economics of the Soviet Union and Eastern Europe.

To those who seek a new grand design for American foreign policy, the changing world environment resulting from the new Soviet policies may offer an unprecedented opportunity to attempt again a bipartisan approach. While all of the conditions leading to a foreign policy consensus after World War II may not exist, some parallels exist. In particular, just as the policy of isolationism was rendered obsolete by technology that brought nations closer together, the post-World War II policies are becoming inadequate to meet current realities. A divided government makes the support of both branches and both parties essential for effective foreign policy. The necessary mutual support may be more likely to develop if both branches and both parties participate in formulating the new policy from the beginning.

To those who seek a specific goal, it is not necessary to limit the concept of a bipartisan foreign policy to a single grand design. It may be possible to construct a bipartisan policy on a particular foreign policy issue, or on several issues individually or in a package, whenever leaders of both branches and both parties believe it is necessary to do so and are willing to seek common ground and make compromises.

The pitfalls of a bipartisan foreign policy in the past need to be recognized. There may have been times when efforts to demonstrate unity prevented adequate debate and criticism of a policy proposal. Dissident voices may have been labeled derogatorily. Policies may have persisted past their time, and new approaches may not have been sought when they were needed. By recognizing these pitfalls, it might be possible to avoid them in any future efforts to formulate a new bipartisan foreign policy.

Meanwhile, even if the assumptions on which foreign policy is based have not been widely shared for many years, enough basic changes have occurred to warrant reexamination of the assumptions. Debate on the significance of new international realities for the national interest of the United States might clarify both the assumptions and the realities. Only after such a debate will it be possible to determine the extent of consensus or any major differences in views.

NOTES TO PART ONE

1. This study has been greatly facilitated by the Congressional Quarterly's publication of key roll call votes that includes a party-breakdown and are collected in its annual Almanac. Specific votes referred to throughout this study have been taken from that publication. Most recent at the time of writing was Congressional Quarterly. Almanac. 100th Congress, 2nd Session... 1988. Vol. XLIV. Washington, Congressional Quarterly, Inc., 1989.

2. In each of the 17 elections from 1888 through 1952, voters gave newly elected Presidents a Congress of the same party, and off-Presidential elections seldom changed the situation. Sayler, James. Politically Divided Government, an Enduring U.S. Problem? CRS Review, June 1989, p. 28.

3. The index was compiled by James McCormick and Eugene Wittkopf based on an analysis of foreign policy roll-call votes in the House and Senate on which the President took a position. McCormick, James M. and Eugene R. Wittkopf. Bipartisanship in Congressional-Executive Relations, 1947-1986, Myth or Reality. Paper prepared for delivery at the Joint Annual Convention of the British International Studies Association and the International Studies Association, London, 28 March-1 April, 1989. Bipartisanship, Partisanship, and Ideology in Congressional-Executive Foreign Policy Relations, 1947-1988. Journal of Politics, November 1990.

4. See Gray, Robert C. Congress, Arms Control, and Weapons Modernization. Congress and Foreign Policy, 1983; and Congress, MX, and Arms Control. Congress and Foreign Policy, 1984. Congress and Foreign Policy is an annual volume prepared by the Congressional Research Service for the House Committee on Foreign Affairs and published as a committee print. Hereinafter referred to as Congress and Foreign Policy, with year.

5. Taft-Morales, Maureen, and Mark P. Sullivan. Congress and Policy toward Central America and Panama, in Congress and Foreign Policy, 1988.

6. Fascell, Dante. Reflections on a Bipartisan Foreign Policy. Miami Herald, Feb. 12, 1989. Reprinted in Congressional Record (daily ed.), April 4, 1989, p. E 1040.

7. U.S. President. (Taft, William Howard.) Annual Message, Part I, Dec. 3, 1912. Messages and Papers of the Presidents, (Richardson) v. XV. New York, Bureau of National Literature, p. 7767.

8. Vandenberg, Arthur Hendrick. Private Papers of Senator Vandenberg. Boston, Houghton Mifflin, 1952. p. 351.

9. Dulles, John Foster. War or Peace. New York, Macmillan, 1950. p. 124.

10. House Republican Policy Committee. What's Left of Bipartisan Foreign Policy? A Policy Analysis with Votes and Quotes. House Republican Policy Committee, October 1988. See esp. p. 105.

11. See Harkins, Daniel F. Uses and Misuses of the Ideas of Consensus and Dissensus in the Analysis of American Foreign Policy: Anticipation, Retrospection, Opinion, and Behavior. Paper Prepared for Delivery at the Joint Annual Convention of the British International Studies Association and the International Studies Association, London, March 29 to April 1, 1989.

12. Lugar, Sen. Richard G. The Direction of American Foreign Policy. Remarks to National Press Club, January 23, 1985. In remarks of Sen. Daniel Quayle, Congressional Record, January 24, 1985, p. S 709. See also Gwertzman, Bernard. Senator Planning Sweeping Hearing of Foreign Policy. New York Times, December 9, 1984, p. A1.

13. A study of Democratic and Republic platforms between 1944 and 1976 found that most of the differences were evident in planks incorporated in the platform by one party but not the other. It found that 34% of the foreign policy topics were bipartisan pledges (this was a higher percentage than any domestic topic except civil rights); 60% were one-party pledges only (this was a lower percentage than any domestic topic), and 6% were conflicting pledges. Pomper, Gerald, with Susan S. Lederman. Elections in America. New York, Longman, 1980, p. 169. Quoted in Wayne, Stephen S. The Road to the White House. New York, St. Martin's, 1988, p. 148-149.

14. Wayne, The Road to the White House, p. 148.

15. Congressional Quarterly, October 22, 1988, p. 3041.

16. On Central America, the Democratic platform spoke of being "deeply disturbed that the current administration has too long abandoned the peace process in the Middle East and consistently undermined it in Central America.... We further believe the United States must fully support the Arias Peace Plan, which calls for an end to the fighting, national reconciliation...an end to support for irregular forces...." The Republican platform said, "Today, thousands of Nicaraguans are united in a struggle to free their homeland from a totalitarian regime. The Republican Party stands shoulder to shoulder with them with both humanitarian and military aid."

On South Africa, the Democratic Platform said the time had come to "declare South Africa a terrorist state, to impose comprehensive sanctions upon its economy, to lead the international community in participation in these actions, and to determine a date certain by which United States corporations must leave South Africa." The Republican platform said "actions designed to pressure the government of South Africa must not have the effect of adversely affecting the rising aspirations and achievements of black South African entrepreneurs and workers and their families."

17. These and excerpts from 1988 platforms in preceding footnote are taken from: Coleman, Kevin J. The 1988 Presidential Election: The Platforms Presented by the Democratic Party (Dukakis/Bentsen) and the Republican Party (Bush/Quayle), with Cross-Referenced Index. CRS Report 88-617 GOV.

18. Vandenberg, Private Papers of Senator Vandenberg, p. 23.

19. Crabb, Cecil V. Jr. Bipartisan Foreign Policy; Myth or Reality? Evanston, Illinois, Row, Peterson and Company, 1957. p. 6.

20. See Hilsman, Roger. Congressional-Executive Relations and the Foreign Policy Consensus. American Political Science Review, September 1968, p. 725-744.

21. Connally, Tom. My Name Is Tom Connally. New York, Thomas Y. Crowell, 1954. p. 261

22. Ibid., p. 254.

23. Notter, Harley. Postwar Foreign Policy Preparation, 1939-1945. Department of State Publication 3580, Washington, GPO, 1950. p. 74.

24. The two opposing votes came from Republican Senators Henrik Shipstead and William Langer.

25. Participants in consultations on aid to Greece and Turkey included Senators Style Bridges, Arthur H. Vandenberg, Wallace H. White, and Robert A. Taft, Republicans, and Tom Connally, Alben W. Barkley, Kenneth D. McKellar, Democrats; and Representatives Joseph H. Martin, Jr., Charles A. Eaton, John Taber, Charles A. Halleck, Republicans, and Sam Rayburn, Sol Bloom, Clarence Cannon, and George H. Mahon, Democrats.

26. Vandenberg, Private Papers of Senator Vandenberg, p. 351, and Crabb, Bipartisan Foreign Policy, p. 60.

27. Participants were Senators Styles Bridges, Arthur H. Vandenberg, Wallace H. White, and Robert A. Taft, and Representatives Leslie Arends, Joseph W. Martin, Jr., Charles A. Eaton, John Taber, Jesse P. Wolcott, and Charles A. Halleck, Republicans; and Senators Tom Connally, Alben W. Barkley, and Scott Lucas, and Representatives Sam Rayburn, Sol Bloom, Clarence Cannon, Democrats. Truman, Harry S. Memoirs, v. 2. Garden City, N.Y., Doubleday, 1956. p. 117.

28. Hutchinson, Martha Crenshaw. The Marshall Plan Model: A Case Study of the Congressional Information Problem. In Executive-Legislative Consultation on Foreign Policy, Strengthening the Legislative Side. Congress and Foreign Policy Series, No. 5. House Foreign Affairs Committee Print, April 1982. p. 84. See also Price, Harry B. The Marshall Plan and Its Meaning. Ithaca, N.Y., Cornell University Press, 1955; and Arkes, Hadley. Bureaucracy, the Marshall Plan, and the National Interest. Princeton University Press, 1972.

29. S. Res. 239, adopted June 11, 1948, by a vote of 64 to 4.

30. U.S. Congress. Senate. Committee on Foreign Relations. Report on the North Atlantic Treaty. Ex. Rept. No. 8, 81st Congress, 1st sess., June 6, 1949.

31. Vandenberg, Private Papers of Senator Vandenberg, p. 519.

32. Crabb, Bipartisan Foreign Policy, p. 104.

33. Cheever, Daniel S., and H. Field Haviland. American Foreign Policy and the Separation of Powers. Cambridge, Harvard University Press, 1952. p. 155.

34. Anderson, David L. China Policy and Presidential Politics, 1952. Presidential Studies Quarterly, v. 10, Winter 1980, p. 83.

35. Congressional Record, June 28, 1950, p. 9319-9323.

36. Connally, My Name Is Tom Connally, p. 350-351.

37. U.S. Congress. Senate. Committee on Foreign Relations. Legislative History, 82nd Congress. Senate Document No. 161, 1952. p. 60.

38. The dissenting vote came from Republican Senator William Langer.

39. The two opposing votes came from Democratic Senators Wayne Morse and Ernest Gruening.

40. Gibbons, William. The U.S. Government and the Vietnam War. Executive and Legislative Roles and Relationships, Part II, 1961-1964. Senate Foreign Relations Committee. S. Prt. 98-185, Pt. 2, p. 314.

41. Department of Defense Appropriations, FY 1970, P.L. 91-171.

42. Section 307 of the Second Supplemental Appropriation Act, Fiscal Year 1973, P.L. 93-50, approved July 1, 1973.

43. Sullivan, Jack. The War Powers Resolution; A Special Study of the Committee on Foreign Affairs. House Foreign Affairs Committee Print, 1982. p. 117-167.

44. P.L. 98-119, approved October 12, 1983.

45. S.J.Res. 159 was passed by both houses on September 29, 1983. The Senate vote was 54-46 (R 52-3; D 2-43.) The House vote was 270-161 (R 140-27; D 130-134.)

46. For additional discussion, see Laipson, Ellen. Congress and the Withdrawal of the Marines from Lebanon. In Congress and Foreign Policy, 1984. p. 11-20.

47. Reagan, President Ronald. Bipartisan Foreign Policy. The Washington Quarterly, White Paper 1984. p. 12.

48. Congressional Record, March 2, 1984, p. S 2214.

49. See Congress and U.S. Policy Toward Central America and the Caribbean, by K. Larry Storrs, in Congress and Foreign Policy, 1982.

50. Serafino, Nina M. Congressional Concerns About U.S. Policy Toward Nicaragua and Honduras. In Congress and Foreign Policy, 1983.

51. Harper, Steven R. Congress and Policy Toward Central America. In Congress and Foreign Policy, 1984.

52. Potter, Anne L. The Battle over Nicaragua. In Congress and Foreign Policy, 1985-86.

53. U.S. Congress. Report of the Congressional Committees Investigating the Iran-Contra Affair, with Supplemental, Minority, and Additional Views. S. Rept. No. 100-216, H. Rept. No. 100-433, 100th Congress, 1st Session, November 1987. p. 4.

54. Robinson, Linda. Congress and U.S. Policy Toward Nicaragua in 1987. In Congress and Foreign Policy, 1987; and Taft-Morales and Sullivan, Congress and Policy Toward Central America and Panama, in Congress and Foreign Policy, 1988.

55. Kissinger, Henry, and Cyrus Vance. Bipartisan Objectives for American Foreign Policy. Foreign Affairs, Summer, 1988, p. 899.

56. U.S. Congress. Senate. Committee on Foreign Relations. Nomination of James A. Baker III. Hearings, Jan. 17 and 18, 1989. p. 12.

57. Boren, David L. and John C. Danforth. Why This Country Can't Lead. Washington Post, December 1, 1987. p. A21.

58. See letter of Carol T. Crawford, Assistant Attorney General, to Hon. Dante B. Fascell, Chairman, Committee on Foreign Affairs, May 31, 1989, and veto message of Senate Joint Resolution 113 to prohibit the export of certain technology, defense articles, and defense services in connection with the codevelopment and coproduction of the FS-X aircraft with Japan. Senate Document 101-14.

59. Rosenthal, Andrew. Above the Dirt Arena, Bush Keeps the Score. New York Times, October 31, 1989, p. A20. Friedman, Thomas L. Baker's World. If Politics Dictate the Secretary's Approach, Some Question the Course of Foreign Policy. New York Times, September 21, 1989, p. A1.

60. New York Times, March 25, 1989, p. A6.

61. Ibid.

62. Draft letter from Secretary of State to Chairmen of House and Senate Authorization and Appropriation Committees and Senate and House leadership. Congressional Record, April 13, 1989, p. H 1194.

63. Under the *Chadha* decision, 462 U.S. 919 (1983), a legislative veto is considered a statutory provision that permits one or both Houses of Congress or a committee to approve or disapprove an executive action without the full legislative process including presentation of the measure to the President for possible veto.

64. The House passed the measure, H.R. 1750, by a vote of 309-110 (D 153-98; R 156-12); the Senate passed it by a vote of 89-9 (D 50-4; R 39-5). Congressional Quarterly, April 15, 1989, p. 853-4.

65. Gallagher, James P., Foreign Affairs Policy Analyst. What's Wrong with the Bipartisan Accord on Central America? Republican Study Committee position paper, in Congressional Record, April 13, 1989, p. H 1193.

66. Friedman, Thomas L. White House Seeks a Pretoria Stance. New York Times, June 28, 1989, p. A5.

67. Africa Insider, September 30, 1989, p. 2.

68. Friedman, White House Seeks a Pretoria Stance, p. A5. See also Raymond W. Copson. South Africa's Future: Toward a Negotiated Settlement? CRS Report 90-302F, June 15, 1990.

69. Ottaway, David B. Bush, Hill Seek Bipartisan Accord on Policy Approach to South Africa. Washington Post, October 1, 1989, p. A20.

70. John Felton, South Africa; Congress Is Willing To Defer Imposing New Sanctions, Congressional Quarterly, October 7, 1989, p. 2659.

71. Boren, David L. Speaking with a Single Voice: Bipartisanship in Foreign Policy. SAID Review, v. 9, Winter/Spring 1989, p. 53.

72. Percy, Charles H. The Partisan Gap. Foreign Policy, Winter 1981-1982, p. 3.

73. New York Times, March 25, 1989, p. A6.

74. Congressional Record, January 5, 1951, p. 55.

75. Falk, Richard. Lifting the Curse of Bipartisanship. World Policy Journal, Fall, 1988, p. 131.

76. Ibid., p. 27.

77. Ibid., p. 129, 156.

78. House Republican Policy Committee, What's Left of Bipartisan Foreign Policy? p. 4, 107.
79. Crabb, Bipartisan Foreign Policy, p. 2.
80. Dulles, War or Peace, p. 122.
81. Clines, Francis X. Is It Bipartisanship or Is It Symbiosis? New York Times, May 16, 1983, p. A14.
82. Corwin, Edward S. The President, Office and Powers, 1787-1957. New York, New York University Press, 1957, p. 17.
83. Dulles, War or Peace, p. 182.
84. Reagan, President. Speech to Georgetown University Center for Strategic and International Studies, April 6, 1984. Washington Post, April 7, 1984, p. A9.
85. Senator Vandenberg was fond of quoting Harold Stassen on this matter, as described in the Private Papers of Senator Vandenberg, p. 230.
86. Bush, George. It Was Never Intended That Foreign Policy Be Reviewed by Grand Juries. Conservative Digest, v. 13, April 1987, p. 55.
87. Message returning without approval Senate Joint Resolution 113, a joint resolution that would prohibit the export of certain technology, defense articles, and defense services in connection with the codevelopment and coproduction of the FS-X aircraft with Japan, July 31, 1989. Senate Document 101-15, September 28, 1989.
88. Letter from Senators Boren, Bradley, Nunn, Boschwitz, Kassebaum, and Danforth. Remarks of Senator Danforth, Congressional Record, March 6, 1989, p. S 2169.
89. U.S. Congress. House. Committee on Foreign Affairs. Required Reports to Congress on Foreign Policy. Prepared by the Foreign Affairs Division, Congressional Research Service, Library of Congress. August 1, 1988. Committee Print. Washington, GPO, 1988, p. iii.
90. Remarks of Senator George McGovern, Congressional Record, May 25, 1978, p. 8298.
91. Destler, I. M. Executive-Congressional Conflict in Foreign Policy; Explaining It, Coping with It. In Dodd, Lawrence C. and Bruce I. Oppenheimer. Congress Reconsidered. 2d ed. Washington, Congressional Quarterly Press, 1981. p. 302.
92. Hughes, Thomas L. The Crack-Up: The Price of Collective Irresponsibility. Foreign Policy, Fall 1980, p. 8. Klingberg, Frank L. Cyclical Trends in American Foreign Policy Moods. Lanham, Maryland, University Press of America, 1983. Elder, Robert E. and Jack E. Holmes. U.S. Foreign Policy Moods Applied to Presidential Personality. In Holmes, Jack E. The Mood/Interest Theory of American Foreign Policy. Lexington, University Press of Kentucky, 1985.
93. Caloss, Dario Jr. The Foreign Policy Belief Systems of Americans: National Idealism and National Self-Interest as Central Value Systems Among the American Public. Prepared for delivery at the 1989 Annual Meeting of the International Studies Association, London, England, March 28-April 1, 1989.
94. McCormick and Wittkopf, Bipartisanship in Congressional-Executive Relations, 1947-1986: Myth or Reality?, p. 21.

95. An exception was President Truman's appointment of General George C. Marshall as Secretary of State in 1947 who reportedly refused to vote during his tenure on grounds his advice should not be tinged by politics. President Truman reportedly told Secretary Marshall, "You tell me about the world, I'll tell you about American politics and what will fly." In Friedman, Baker's World, p. A18.

96. See remarks of Rep. Robert S. Walker (Pa.), and Rep. Newt Gingrich, Congressional Record, May 8, 1984, p. H 3537-3556.

97. *Lowry v. Reagan*, 676 F. Supp. 333 (D.D.C. 1987).

98. Huckshorn, Robert J. Political Parties in America. Monterey, California, Brooks/Cole Publishing Company, 1984, p. 277.

99. U.S. Congress. House. Committee on International Relations (Foreign Affairs). Special Subcommittee on Investigations. Congress and Foreign Policy. Report, January 2, 1977. Kendrick, Joseph T. The Consultation Process--The Legislative-Executive Relationship in the Formulation of Foreign Policy. Doctoral dissertation submitted to George Washington University, May 6, 1979, p. 133.

100. Collier, Ellen C. Strengthening Executive-Legislative Consultation on Foreign Policy. Congress and Foreign Policies Series, No. 8. U.S. Congress. House Foreign Affairs Committee Print, October 1983, p. 1.

101. See also section below, Attitudinal Requirements.

102. Westerfield, H. Bradford. Foreign Policy and Party Politics, Pearl Harbor to Korea. New York, Octagon Books, 1972. p. 12-13.

103. Fascell, Dante. Congress and the Challenges of Our Third Century. Congressional Record, March 8, 1988, p. E 569. See also discussion of current efforts to establish a consultation group, in section above, Fresh Effort at Bipartisan Foreign Policy.

104. See chapter, Congress, Arms Control, and Weapons Modernization, by Robert C. Gray, in Congress and Foreign Policy, 1983.

105. Schmitt, Gary J. Why Commissions Don't Work. The National Interest, Spring 1989, p. 60.

106. See chapters: Congress and the Central America-Caribbean Region, by K. Larry Storrs, in Congress and Foreign Policy, 1983, and Congress and Policy toward Central American, by Steven R. Harper, in Congress and Foreign Policy, 1984.

107. U.S. Congress. House. Committee on Foreign Affairs. Report of the Task Force on Foreign Assistance. House Document 101-32. February 1989. 43 p.

108. Schmitt, Why Commissions Don't Work, p. 66.

109. The Democrats appointed Edward King and Kirk O'Donnell; the Republicans appointed the Rev. Ira Galloway and Jeane Kirkpatrick. Robinson, Congress and U.S. Policy Toward Nicaragua in 1987, in Congress and Foreign Policy, 1987.

110. The Commission was established by Public Law 94-304, signed June 3, 1976.

111. U.S. Library of Congress. Congressional Research Service. Conference on Security and Cooperation in Europe (CSCE): After the Vienna Meeting, by Francis T. Miko. Issue Brief IB87220. July 17, 1989.

112. These examples are taken from Crabb, Bipartisan Foreign Policy, p. 35-41.
113. Congressional Record, April 13, 1989, p. S 3975.
114. Congressional Record, April 13, 1989, p. S 3976.
115. U.S. Congress. House. Committee on Foreign Affairs. Report of the Task Force on Foreign Assistance.
116. See Report of the Congressional Committees Investigating the Iran-Contra Affair with Supplemental, Minority, and Additional Views. See also chapter, Congress and the Iran-Contra Affair, by Joel Woldman, in Congress and Foreign Policy, 1987.
117. Public Law 79-601, sec. 202.
118. U.S. Congress. Senate. Foreign Relations Committee. Background Information on the Committee on Foreign Relations, January 1966, p. 27.
119. Public Law 91-510, Sec. 301 (a).
120. U.S. Congress. Senate. Committee on Foreign Relations. 170th Anniversary, 1816-1986. Washington, GPO, 1986, p. 39.
121. Ibid., p. 40
122. Congressional Record, October 13, 1980, p. S 14397.
123. Destler, Executive-Congressional Conflict in Foreign Policy, p. 307.
124. Ibid., p. 309.
125. Pell, Senator Claiborne. Remarks at Woman's National Democratic Club, February 28, 1989. In Congressional Record, April 4, 1989, p. S 3263.
126. Congressional Record, January 5, 1951, p. 55.
127. Bicentennial Minute: February 26, (1919): Foreign Relations Committee at White House. Congressional Record (daily ed.), February 26, 1987, p. S 2406.
128. Congressional Record, March 18, 1987, p. 2167.
129. Congressional Record, February 22, 1989. Washington's Farewell Address is read annually in its entirety in the United States Senate on Washington's birthday, February 22.

PART TWO

Documents on Bipartisan Foreign Policymaking

Models of Making Bipartisan Foreign Policy

**Charter of the United Nations;
Report of the Senate Foreign Relations
Committee, July 16, 1945 (Excerpts)**[1]

The Committee on Foreign Relations, having had under consideration Executive F, Seventy-ninth Congress, first session, the Charter of the United Nations, with the Statute of the International Court of Justice annexed thereto, formulated at the United Nations Conference on International Organization and signed in San Francisco on June 26, 1945, hereby report the same favorably to the Senate without amendment and recommend that the Senate advise and consent to the ratification thereof.

Submission of the Charter by the President

The President of the United States appeared before the Senate on July 2, 1945, to submit the Charter and the Statute for approval....

Contribution of the American People

During the course of his address the President pointed out that the principles on which it is based "are not new to the United States Senate or to the House of Representatives," since the Charter is in complete accord with the Connally resolution adopted by the Senate in November 1943, and with the

Fulbright resolution previously adopted by the House of Representatives. Both the President and the witnesses who testified before the committee emphasized the important contributions which have been made by the Congress and the American people to the formulation of the Charter of the United Nations.

During the 6 years preceding the San Francisco Conference our Government made exhaustive study of every aspect of our postwar foreign policy, including the whole problem of international organization. Under the constant leadership and wise guidance of President Roosevelt and Secretary Hull a number of advisory committees, composed of Members of both Houses of the Congress, high officials of the State, War, and Navy Departments, and many outstanding private citizens, studied for a period of 3 years all questions relating to the establishment of an international organization.

As a result of long, thorough preparatory work and in view of developing public opinion--as exemplified by the Fulbright resolution, the Ball-Burton-Hatch-Hill resolution, and the Connally resolution, and by the Mackinac resolution adopted by the Republican Party in September 1943--Secretary Hull joined with representatives of China, the Soviet Union, and the United Kingdom on October 31, 1943, in issuing the Moscow declaration, in which the four Governments called for the establishment of an international organization for the maintenance of peace and security and pledged themselves to work together for the creation of such an organization.

The preparatory work and wide consultation culminated in an American draft proposal which was submitted to the British, Soviet, and Chinese Governments on July 18, 1944. Thereafter, these Governments also submitted corresponding proposals and the four documents constituted the basis of the Dumbarton Oaks conversations which took place in Washington from August 21 to October 7, 1944. At the Crimea Conference in February 1945, the proposals formulated at Dumbarton Oaks were further elaborated.

During the 6 months preceding the San Francisco Conference the Dumbarton Oaks proposals were studied and debated extensively by the American people. Many valuable comments and suggestions were submitted which were helpful to the United States delegation to the Conference.

At various times during the elaboration of these proposals the executive branch of the Government consulted with a nonpartisan group of members of the Foreign Relations Committee headed by the chairman and including Senators George, Barkley, Gillette, Thomas of Utah, Vandenberg, White, Austin, and La Follette.

The nonpartisan character of the support throughout the country for our participation in an international organization to maintain peace was further emphasized by the specific declarations on this subject found in the Democratic and Republican Party platforms of 1944.

Forty-two national organizations were invited to send representatives to San Francisco to serve as consultants to the delegation. These consultants made important contributions to the drafting of the Charter.

Hearings

The committee began its consideration of the Charter and the Statute on July 9, 1945....

The chairman of the United States delegation to the San Francisco Conference, the Honorable Edward R. Stettinius, Jr., was the first witness invited to appear before the committee. In his statement...Mr. Stettinius declared that he wished "to make full acknowledgment of the great part taken by Members of Congress, and particularly by Members of the United States Senate, in making this Charter possible and in framing its provision." Mr. Stettinius then commented on the contributions to the Charter made by Members of the Congress and by the American people as a whole:

> Half of the United States delegation at the San Francisco Conference was composed of Members of Congress. Your chairman, Senator Connally, and his distinguished colleague, Senator Vandenberg, acted as vice chairmen of the delegation. They played outstanding roles in the writing of this Charter. They were leading figures at the United

Nations Conference and their contributions to its success did honor to themselves, to the Senate, and to the country.

I wish also to pay high tribute to Representative Bloom, whom I am happy to see here today, and Congressman Eaton, who I wish could be here, who represented the House with such distinction, and to the two able and influential public members of the delegation, Dean Gildersleeve and Commander Stassen. Mr. Hull, whom President Roosevelt rightly called "the father of the United Nations" was not present, but we were in daily communication with him and his wise counsel was invaluable. Finally, President Truman, your colleague for so many years, guided our efforts with clear vision and a sure hand. His leadership contributed greatly to our success.

From first to last Congress and the executive branch of the Government have worked hand in hand and with no thought of partisanship in this great endeavor. The whole American people have also participated directly to an extent never approached before. The Dumbarton Oaks proposals were submitted to their scrutiny, criticism and advice 7 months before the San Francisco Conference began, and the results of that public examination are reflected in many of the changes made at San Francisco. Forty-two nongovernmental organizations representing labor, agriculture, industry, the churches, veterans, and other groups were represented by consultants to the United States delegation at the Conference. They, too, exercised an important influence in the construction of the Charter....

During the course of his testimony Mr. Stettinius stated that both the War and Navy Departments had certified that they were of the opinion that the military and strategic implications of the Charter as a whole are in accord with the security interests of the United States....

After the committee had heard the testimony of Mr. Stettinius it invited Dr. Leo Pasvolsky, special assistant to the Secretary of State for international organization and security affairs and one of the advisers of the United States delegation at the Conference, to analyze the Charter of the United Nations, article by article. Dr. Pasvolsky was chairman of the coordination committee of the Conference, which was responsible for the final drafting of the Charter and the Statute. The committee then called upon Mr. Green H. Hackworth, legal adviser of the Department of State and one of the advisers of the United States delegation at the Conference. Mr. Hackworth, who presided over the committee of jurists which met in Washington from April 9 to April 20, 1945, inclusive, and who took an important part in the committee at the San Francisco Conference which dealt with the International Court of Justice, went over in detail the provisions of the Statute of the proposed Court. Throughout their testimony Dr. Pasvolsky and Mr. Hackworth were questioned constantly by members of your committee and by other Members of the Senate who were present. The principal issues which were discussed during this period of the committee's hearings are summarized later in this report.

The committee invited testimony from anyone who wished to comment favorably or unfavorably upon the Charter and the Statute. During the period July 11-13, 1945, when full opportunity was given to all persons who wished to testify, the committee heard a total of 60 witnesses, including Mr. John Foster Dulles, of New York, who acted as an adviser to the United States delegation at the San Francisco Conference. No one who requested permission to appear and testify was denied an opportunity to do so, and written statements for the record were freely accepted from all sources. There were read into the record of the committee a large number of telegrams from individuals and organizations and many newspaper editorials, the great majority of which wholeheartedly endorsed the Charter. The committee was impressed by the fact that very little opposition was expressed to the Charter and to participation in the Organization by the United States....

Conclusion

The committee is satisfied that the Charter represents a remarkable accomplishment in the process of developing international cooperation. While it may be that this is not a perfect instrument, the important thing is that agreement has been reached on this particular Charter, after months and even years of careful study and negotiation, between the representatives of 50 nations. The virtual unanimity with which the results of the Dumbarton Oaks and the San Francisco Conferences have been approved by the people of the United States and now by this committee, is the best proof now available that a sound and practicable foundation has been achieved on which to work for peace and security....

The question of our membership in an international organization to preserve peace has been debated throughout our country and in this Congress as fully as any public issue in our history has ever been discussed. The committee feels that the people and the members of the Senate understand clearly the consequences and the requirements of our membership in the United Nations and that they are prepared to undertake the responsibilities of membership in order to enjoy the privileges which that membership may ultimately bring in the form of world security. The committee is convinced that participation in the United Nations is in accordance with our national interests, and that our contributions to the United Nations will be repaid many times.

The committee, therefore, has no hesitation in recommending that the Senate advise and consent to the ratification of the Charter of the United Nations....

European Recovery Program;
Report of the Senate Foreign Relations Committee,
February 27, 1948 (Excerpts)[2]

The Committee on Foreign Relations, having had under consideration a bill (S. 2202) to promote the general welfare, national interest, and foreign policy of the United States through necessary economic and financial assistance to foreign countries, unanimously report the bill favorably to the Senate, without amendment, and recommend that it do pass....

1. Events Leading Up to the Present Situation

During the summer of 1947, when UNRRA expired, Europe had not achieved a condition of economic and political stability. Not only did the extreme cold of last winter curtail European crops, but they were even more severely affected by the severe drought of the summer just passed. Moreover, the international monetary system was thrown out of balance by the rapidly rising cost of imports and the suspension of the convertibility of the pound sterling. These developments made it particularly difficult for the countries of Europe to secure needed supplies.

In order to alleviate immediate suffering and to pave the way for later long-range action, on November 17, 1947, President Truman called Congress into special session to deal with "the rise in prices...(and)...the crisis in western Europe." Congress met his request in December and provided funds for interim aid to France, Italy and Austria until April 1, 1948, when it was expected that the long-range program would be in operation.

The present legislation was anticipated by two addresses, one by Under Secretary of State Dean Acheson, on May 8, 1947, the second by Secretary of State George C. Marshall, on June 5, 1947, in which both indicated that the United States stood ready to consider how far she might be able to help Europe help herself on the road to recovery. On July 11, 1947, 16 western European nations on their own initiative responded to the suggestion, and met in Paris to prepare a report setting forth their needs and their willingness to cooperate in a joint recovery program. Meanwhile, United States agencies, Members of Congress traveling abroad, and special committees appointed by the President, studied the needs of the European nations, and the impact of the contemplated assistance upon our resources and upon our domestic economy. On December 19, 1947, President Truman sent his special message to Congress on the situation in Europe, requesting relief in the amount of $17,000,000,000 for a period to run from April 1, 1948, to June 30, 1952, with a recommendation for an appropriation of $6,800,000,000 for the 15-month period running from April 1, 1948, to June 30, 1949. The President also made a number of recommendations as to administration, the types of agreements to be made, and the financial arrangements which were to be embodied in the new program.

2. The Committee Hearings

The committee conducted hearings on the European recovery program from January 8 to February 5, inclusive. On January 8, Secretary of State George C. Marshall accompanied by Ambassador Lewis W. Douglas and members of the State Department staff presented the program in general terms and urged the speedy passage of the draft bill which he presented for legislative consideration. On following days Ambassador Douglas returned to analyze in detail the political, economic, and administrative problems involved in a recovery program.

On January 12, Secretary of Commerce W. Averell Harriman presented the findings of the Harriman committee, discussing in detail the impact of the program upon the United States economy and other related matters. On January 13 Secretary of Agriculture Clinton P. Anderson described the food and agricultural parts of the recommended program and pointed out what they would mean to the farmers and consumers of the United States. On the same day Secretary of the Interior Julius A. Krug presented an analysis of the findings of the Krug committee on national resources and foreign aid with particular emphasis upon the effect of the recovery program upon certain commodities in short supply.

On January 14 Secretary of the Treasury John W. Snyder discussed the principal financial aspects of the program and the measures the participating countries would be expected to take. Mr. William M. Martin, Jr. explained the possible role of the Export-Import Bank in such a program. On the same day Secretary of the Army Kenneth C. Royall discussed the role of Germany in the rehabilitation of the European economy and the relationship of the European recovery program to the national defense. The list of Government witnesses was completed on January 15 when Secretary of Defense James V. Forrestal described the relationship of the recovery program to the security interests of the United States.

During the 3 weeks that followed, nearly 100 nongovernmental witnesses appeared before the committee. Included were representatives of many of our outstanding national organizations, spokesmen of business, labor, agricultural, veterans, religious, educational, and service groups. Included also were many outstanding individuals who appeared in their capacity as private citizens, such as John Foster Dulles, Bernard Baruch, and Robert M. La Follette.

Following the conclusion of the public hearings the committee met in executive session for an additional week to continue its consideration of the European recovery program, taking as a basis for discussion the draft proposal submitted by the Department of State. On the basis of information obtained during the hearings the committee proceeded to rewrite the bill, essentially altering it in many important particulars. On February 17 the committee concluded its deliberations and voted unanimously to report the bill favorably to the Senate.

As in the case of the Foreign Aid Act, the committee was greatly impressed with the thorough documentation which was available during its examination of the European recovery program. It is probable that no legislative proposal coming before the Congress has ever been accompanied by such thoroughly prepared documentary materials. In addition to the extensive documents submitted by the Department of State, the reports of the Paris Conference of the CEEC countries, the Nourse, Krug, and Harriman reports, the handbook on the European recovery program prepared by the staffs of the Senate

Foreign Relations Committee and the House Foreign Affairs Committee, the special report of the Brookings Institution, and the numerous reports of the House Select Committee on Foreign Aid were all available. Added to these reports was a great deal of material which had been produced in the course of congressional experience with foreign-aid matters prior to 1948, such as discussions relating to UNRRA, interim aid, etc.

Particular reference should be made at this point to the report submitted by the Brookings Institution. Early in its consideration of the European recovery program it became apparent to the committee that the task of providing for a satisfactory administrative organization for such an important program would be extremely difficult. Accordingly, the Chairman of the Foreign Relations Committee invited the Brookings Institution to analyze the various proposals which had been advanced and to submit its findings and recommendations. On January 22 this report was completed. It served as a basis of discussion for the members of the committee and helped them arrive at a satisfactory solution.

The committee was likewise impressed by the fact that very few opposition witnesses appeared to testify against the bill. Representatives of labor and management alike warmly endorsed its objectives. All witnesses were heard who asked to be heard....

15. *The Public Advisory Board*

Because of the broad range of problems involved in the recovery program, the committee believed it highly desirable to create a public advisory board to advise with the Administrator with respect to basic policy matters. Two direct benefits will flow from such an arrangement. In the first place, an advisory board made up of eminent citizens with varied experiences and representing various interests, will be able to contribute many valuable suggestions and criticisms for the use of the Administrator. He will undoubtedly wish to lean heavily upon their counsel. In the second place, if the Administrator works closely with an advisory body consisting of representatives of labor, business, agriculture, and other interested groups, public confidence in the enterprise will be greatly augmented.

As provided in the bill the Public Advisory Council will be bipartisan and will consist of not more than 12 members appointed by the President and confirmed by the Senate. As the name indicates it is to function in an advisory capacity only. The act provides that it shall meet at least once a month and at other times upon the call of the Administrator or the request of three or more of the Board members. The committee sincerely believes the Board will prove a valuable asset to the Administrator without constituting a burden upon his time.

The Administrator is also authorized to appoint such other advisory committees as he may consider necessary to carry out the purposes of the act. It is very probable, as the recovery program progresses, that the Administrator will find special advisory groups in industry, labor, agriculture, commerce, and other specialized fields of considerable assistance to him.

16. The Joint Congressional Committee

The European recovery program will be a gigantic enterprise. It will involve the cooperation and the resources of the United States. Its outcome will determine, to a very large extent, whether peace and prosperity will prevail in the western world. Its successful execution will be of continuing interest to the executive branch, the Congress, and the people of the United States for the next 4 years.

For these reasons the committee believed it would be highly desirable to establish a congressional committee to be known as the Joint Committee on Foreign Economic Cooperation. This joint committee will be bipartisan in character and will be made up of seven Members of the Senate and seven Members of the House. Its chairman and vice chairman will be appointed by the President of the Senate and the Speaker of the House acting jointly.

It will be the task of the joint committee to make a continuous study of United States foreign-aid programs and to review the progress achieved in the execution and administration of such programs. It will also, upon request, aid the standing committees of the Congress having legislative jurisdiction over the various aspects of foreign economic assistance. Finally, it will report to the Congress from time to time making such recommendations as it may deem desirable.

After careful consideration of the issues involved, the committee agreed that it would be most inadvisable to bestow legislative authority upon the joint committee. The recovery program will have many facets, both international and domestic. It will be related to foreign policy, shipping problems, export controls, farm production, stock piling, foreign trade, and financial policy--to mention only a few. To grant the joint committee legislative authority would compel it to invade the proper jurisdiction of many of the standing committees of the Congress.

The committee felt strongly, however, that the joint committee will serve as a useful mechanism to bridge the gap between the executive and legislative branches and thus help bring about the teamwork within our own government which is essential if the program is to succeed. It is believed that the joint committee can play a very helpful role both in keeping the Congress informed and in advancing healthy criticisms and helpful suggestions for the use of the Administrator. The bill provides that the Administrator, at the request of the joint committee, shall consult with the committee from time to time with respect to his activities....

54. Conclusion

On February the 13 the committee concluded its deliberations and unanimously voted to report the bill to the Senate for favorable action.

The committee believes that the program proposed is a sound one, that it will impose no dangerous strain upon the economy of the United States, and that it will be adequate to provide the margin for success in an effort which must be essentially and primarily European.

This kind of assistance, in peacetime, is without precedent in the history of mankind. This assistance is not, and cannot be, a permanent feature of American foreign policy. For Americans, the approval of this act represents a major decision. If Europeans fully understand this decision, they will realize that the United States is making adjustments almost as severe as they are likely to call upon each other to make. Above the details of the legislation, the debates, the statistics, and the work sheets, it is the expression of a great ideal of common welfare and peace. This ideal must become the common currency among the peoples of the world.

North Atlantic Treaty;
Report of the Senate Foreign Relations
Committee, June 6, 1949 (Excerpts)[3]

The Committee on Foreign Relations, to whom was referred the North Atlantic Treaty (Executive L, 81st Cong., 1st sess.), signed at Washington on April 4, 1949, unanimously report the treaty to the Senate and recommend that its advice and consent to ratification be given at an early date....

1. Main Purpose of the Treaty

The basic objective of the treaty is to assist in achieving the primary purpose of the United Nations--the maintenance of peace and security. It is designed to do so by making clear the determination of the members of the North Atlantic community to safeguard their common heritage of freedom by exercising collectively their inherent right of self-defense in the event of an armed attack upon any of them, while making clear at the same time their determination to live in peace with all governments and all peoples....

3. Background of Treaty

The paramount desire of the American people is and always has been for peace and freedom. Since 1776 they have constantly striven, and sometimes fought, to maintain their own freedom and to further the development of freedom elsewhere. They have always sought to live in peace with all men.

Since 1823, when the Monroe Doctrine was promulgated, this Government has contributed to the peace and freedom of the Americas by making clear that it would regard an armed attack upon any part of the Americas as an attack upon the United States. No other doctrine has become more deeply imbedded in American foreign policy. In 1947 all the American Republics joined in signing the Treaty of Rio de Janeiro, which provided that each would regard an attack on any one of them as an attack upon all.

Since World War II. In 1945 the United States Government and the American people wholeheartedly accepted the obligations of the Charter of the United Nations. In so doing they undertook the obligation not to use force except in conformity with the Charter and the responsibility, not only of living up to that obligation but of using their influence to see that other powers live up to it. No government has labored harder or more unceasingly to reach international understanding through the United Nations and to make the United Nations a more effective instrument.

Unfortunately one great power and a small group of nations under its domination have not only refused to cooperate in the establishment of a just and lasting peace, but have sought to prevent it, both within and without the United Nations. That power and its fifth columns in other countries have sought to prevent the establishment of such a peace. It has sought to obstruct efforts for the promotion of human welfare and stability in order to profit from human misery and hunger in propagating its own system and advancing its own imperialistic ends.

This threat to free institutions everywhere has caused free nations to draw together in increased cooperation for both defense and economic recovery, as reflected in the Brussels Treaty and the Convention for European Economic Cooperation. The United States Government, in giving effect to the desire of the American people to assist in promoting peace and freedom, has taken far-reaching steps to this end in the act to provide for assistance to Greece and Turkey and in the European recovery program of 1948 and 1949.

Senate Resolution 239.--The concern of the American people at the unfavorable trend of postwar developments led to the introduction into the Senate during the Eightieth Congress of a large number of resolutions which aspired to change the United Nations Charter or to chart a more effective course for United States foreign policy through the United Nations. The committee thoroughly canvassed the issues involved, in close cooperation with the Department of State, and, on May 19, 1948, unanimously approved Senate Resolution 239, which sought to focus these aspirations on the most constructive measures it considered practicable.

That resolution was adopted by the Senate on June 11, 1948, by a vote of 46-4. It advised the President--

> of the sense of the Senate that this Government, by constitutional process, should particularly pursue the following objectives within the United Nations Charter:
>
>> (1) Voluntary agreement to remove the veto from all questions involving pacific settlements of international disputes and situations, and from the admission of new members.
>> (2) Progressive development of regional and other collective arrangements for individual and collective self-defense in accordance with the purposes, principles, and provisions of the Charter.
>> (3) Association of the United States, by constitutional process, with such regional and other collective arrangements as are based on continuous and effective self-help and mutual aid, and as affect its national security.
>> (4) Contributing to the maintenance of peace by making clear its determination to exercise the right of individual or collective self-defense under article 51 should any armed attack occur affecting its national security.
>> (5) Maximum efforts to obtain agreements to provide the United Nations with armed forces as provided by the Charter, and to obtain agreement among member nations upon universal regulation and reduction of armaments under adequate and dependable guaranty against violation.
>> (6) If necessary, after adequate effort toward strengthening the United Nations, review of the Charter at an appropriate time by a General Conference called under article 109 or by the General Assembly.

Pursuant to this advice the President in July authorized the Secretary of State to enter into exploratory conversations on the security of the North Atlantic area with representatives of the Governments of Belgium, Canada, France, Luxembourg, the Netherlands, and the United Kingdom. These conversations resulted in October in agreement that the establishment by treaty of a collective defense arrangement for the North Atlantic area within the framework of the United Nations Charter was desirable and necessary. The North Atlantic Treaty was accordingly negotiated and signed on April 4, 1949, by representatives of the seven governments which had participated in the initial conversations and of the Governments of Norway, Denmark, Iceland, Italy, and Portugal.

Executive-legislative cooperation.--The committee commends the close cooperation between the executive branch and the Senate, which has characterized the development of this treaty from inception to conclusion as an example of how important matters in the field of foreign relations should be handled. First the committee and the Department of State considered together the problems facing the United States in this field and the courses of action best suited to deal with them. The Senate then gave the President its advice as to particular objectives to be sought. The executive branch faithfully followed the advice of the Senate and, during the negotiations with the other governments, consulted fully with the committee, which played an effective part in formulating the terms of the treaty. From the beginning the deliberations of both the committee and the Senate on Senate Resolution 239 and the treaty have been conducted on a wholly nonpartisan basis. Finally, in order to give the American and other peoples the earliest possible opportunity to consider the treaty, its terms were made public considerably in advance of signature, as soon as they had been agreed upon by the negotiating governments.

4. Committee Hearings and Action

The committee discussed with the Secretary of State the draft of the North Atlantic Treaty in two informal executive meetings on February 8 and March 8. The treaty, made public on March 18, was signed in Washington on April 4, and was transmitted to the Senate on April 12. Before commencing public hearings the committee met again on April 21 to consider the relationship of the treaty to the proposed military-assistance program. Public hearings, beginning on April 27, were held on 16 days--April 27-29, May 2-6, 9-13, and 16-18. Besides the committee members, various Senators attended or participated in the cross-examination of the witnesses. The very extensive and thorough hearings comprise three printed volumes.

The first administration witness was Secretary of State Dean G. Acheson on April 27, 1949. The Hon. Warren R. Austin, Chief, United States Mission to the United Nations; Hon. Louis Johnson, Secretary of Defense; Hon. W. A. Harriman, United States special representative in Europe of the Economic Cooperation Administration; Hon. Robert A. Lovett, former Under Secretary of State, and Gen. Omar N. Bradley, Chief of Staff of the United States Army and representing the Joint Chiefs of Staff, completed the testimony presented for the administration by May 3.

In the succeeding weeks the committee heard all witnesses who requested to be heard. Among the 90 nongovernmental witnesses were representatives from a number of our important business, labor, agricultural, church, veterans, and service groups. In addition, the committee also received communications from organizations, such as the American Federation of Labor, the United States Chamber of Commerce, and the Junior Chamber of Commerce, placing them on record as favoring the treaty.

Following the conclusion of public hearings, the committee met in executive session on June 2 and 6 to evaluate the evidence gained in committee hearings and to consider the committee report. On June 6 the committee voted unanimously (13-0) to report the treaty favorably to the Senate with the recommendation that it be approved for ratification....

Article 5--Action in the Event of Armed Attack...

President and Congress. During the hearings substantially the following questions were repeatedly asked: In view of the provision in article 5 that an attack against one shall be considered an attack against all, would the United States be obligated to react to an attack on Paris or Copenhagen in the same way it would react to an attack on New York City? In such an event does the treaty give the President the power to take any action, without specific congressional authorization, which he could not take in the absence of the treaty?

The answer to both these questions is "No." An armed attack upon any State of the United States by its very nature would require the immediate application of all force necessary to repel the attack. The Constitution itself recognizes the special significance of such a calamity by providing that the United States shall protect each State against invasion. Similarly, the government of any nation party to the treaty would feel itself under obligation and under imminent physical need to give the highest priority to essential countermeasures to meet an armed attack upon its own homeland.

In the event any party to the treaty were attacked the obligation of the United States Government would be to decide upon and take forthwith the measures it deemed necessary to restore and maintain the security of the North Atlantic area. The measures which would be necessary to accomplish that end would depend upon a number of factors, including the location, nature, scale, and significance of the attack. The decision as to what action was necessary, and the action itself, would of course have to be taken in accordance with established constitutional procedures as the treaty in article 11 expressly requires.

Article 5 records what is a fact, namely, that an armed attack within the meaning of the treaty would in the present-day world constitute an attack upon the entire community comprising the parties to the treaty, including the United States. Accordingly, the President and the Congress, within their sphere of assigned constitutional responsibilities, would be expected to take all action necessary and appropriate to protect the United States against the consequences and dangers of an armed attack committed against any party to the Treaty. The committee does not believe it appropriate in this report to undertake to define the authority of the President to use the armed forces. Nothing in the treaty, however, including the provision that an attack against one shall be considered an attack against all, increases or decreases the constitutional powers of either the President or the Congress or changes the relationship between them....

Japanese Peace Treaty and Other Treaties Relating to Security in the Pacific; Report of the Senate Foreign Relations Committee, February 14, 1952 (Excerpts)[4]

The Committee on Foreign Relations, to whom was referred the treaty of peace with Japan (Executive A, 82d Cong., 2d sess.), signed at San Francisco on September 8, 1951; the mutual defense treaty between the United States and the Republic of the Philippines (Executive B, 82d Cong., 2d sess.), signed at Washington on August 30, 1951; the security treaty between Australia, New Zealand, and the United States of America (Executive C, 82d Cong., 2d sess.), signed at San Francisco on September 1, 1951; and the security treaty between the United States of America and Japan (Executive D, 82d Cong., 2d sess.), signed at San Francisco on September 8, 1951, unanimously reports the treaties to the Senate and recommends that its advice and consent to ratification be given at an early date....

2. *Negotiation of the Treaties*

The United States was given the sole responsibility of appointing a supreme commander for all the Allied Powers and directing the occupation of Japan. An obligation to bring the occupation to a timely end also fell upon the United States. To this end, the United States as early as 1947 made overtures for a peace treaty to be considered in the Far Eastern Commission. Persistent opposition from the Soviet Union, partly on the grounds that only the Council of Foreign Ministers, where the Soviet Union exercises a veto, should have jurisdiction over negotiations, successfully blocked all efforts to negotiate a treaty until the fall of 1950. At that time, the United States entered into conversations with former Allied Powers outside the Soviet orbit for the purpose of determining if, in fact, a treaty could be concluded. Frequent consultations took place between the interested delegations during the session of the United Nations General Assembly in New York in 1950.

Representatives of the British Commonwealth worked together to determine their individual and collective position on the basic principles of the treaty, while a mission dispatched by the President of the United States visited the capital cities of the 10 countries most directly concerned for an on-the-spot exchange of views. All recognized the importance of making peace promptly, and agreement was reached on many of the principal objectives. On January 11, 1951, the President designated Mr. John Foster Dulles as his special representative, with the personal rank of Ambassador, to conduct on behalf of the United States such further discussions and negotiations as would be necessary to bring to an eventual successful conclusion a Japanese peace settlement. The United States drew up the first draft of a treaty, embodying these objectives in March 1951, and this was circulated among members of the Far Eastern Commission and other nations that had indicated their interest, including some of Latin America. In all, there was a total of 20.

An outgrowth of the conferences among the members of the British Commonwealth was a draft treaty prepared by the United Kingdom. In June, the two drafts were combined in a text jointly agreed upon by the United States and the United Kingdom and shortly thereafter circulated among the Allied Powers including the U.S.S.R. The middle of August was set as the deadline for incorporating changes.

The United States delegation to the Japanese Peace Conference held in San Francisco last September included a group of Senators and Congressmen. Senators Connally and Wiley were named as delegates for each of the four treaties. Alternate delegates for the Japanese Peace Treaty were Senators John J. Sparkman, H. Alexander Smith, Walter F. George, and Bourke B. Hickenlooper, and Representatives James P. Richards and Robert B. Chiperfield. Alternate delegates for the security treaties with the Philippines and with Australia and New Zealand were Senators John J. Sparkman, H. Alexander Smith, Walter F. George, and Bourke B. Hickenlooper, and Representatives Abraham A. Ribicoff and Walter H. Judd. Alternate delegates for the security treaty with Japan were Senators Richard B. Russell, Styles Bridges, John J. Sparkman, and H. Alexander Smith, and Representatives Overton Brooks and

Dewey Short. Senator Pat McCarran and Representatives Karl Stefan and John J. Rooney served as observers.

The committee wishes to express its appreciation for the cooperative spirit in which the treaties were negotiated by the executive branch of the Government. Rarely, if ever, have committee members seen such legislative-executive teamwork as that which characterized negotiation of the treaties. The committee particularly desires to commend Ambassador Dulles for his outstanding contribution to the cause of world peace and bipartisan consultation.

Eleven months of exhaustive effort by the Allied Powers resulted in a treaty which manifested their desire for a just and lasting peace and which manifested also a subordination of individual interests to the common good.

3. *Committee Action*

January 12, 1951, marked the beginning of a series of meetings, nine in all, between Ambassador Dulles and members of the consultative Subcommittee on Far Eastern Affairs of the Foreign Relations Committee. The meetings continued at frequent intervals throughout the spring and summer, with Ambassador Dulles keeping the subcommittee currently informed of the progress of his negotiations with the Japanese and with the former Allied Powers, until the conclusion and signature of the peace treaty and related security pacts at San Francisco in September. Moreover, on several occasions, Ambassador Dulles discussed with the full committee specific problems that arose during the process of negotiations. Committee suggestions on these problems were instrumental in determining the final text of the treaties.

Upon the reconvening of the Congress after the fall adjournment, President Truman, on January 10, 1952, submitted the treaties with his recommendation that the Senate give them "early favorable consideration."

As a consequence, public hearings began on January 21, with statements by Secretary of State Dean Acheson, Gen. Omar Bradley, Chairman, Joint Chiefs of Staff, and Ambassador

Dulles. Ambassador Dulles returned on the following day to answer questions of committee members. Hearings continued on January 23 and 25, with private witnesses both in opposition to and support of the treaties. Among those offering testimony were representatives of various organizations as well as individuals expressing their own views. In addition, a number of statements were filed with the committee for the record.

At its executive session February 5, the committee, by a vote of 13 to 0, agreed to report all the treaties favorably to the Senate. At that time committee members approved an interpretative statement making clear the position of the Senate with respect to the Yalta agreement and the territorial provisions of the Japanese Peace Treaty. The unanimous vote which the committee gave the four treaties reflected the close cooperation which took place between the committee and the executive branch throughout the negotiations....

Bipartisan Accord on Central America, March 24, 1989[5]

The Executive and the Congress are united today in support of democracy, peace, and security in Central America. The United States supports the peace and democratization process and the goals of the Central American Presidents embodied in the Esquipulas Accord. The United States is committed to working in good faith with the democratic leaders of Central America and Latin America to translate the bright promises of Esquipulas II into concrete realities on the ground.

With regard to Nicaragua, the United States is united in its goals: democratization; an end to subversion and destabilization of its neighbors; an end to Soviet bloc military ties that threaten U.S. and regional security. Today the Executive and the Congress are united on a policy to achieve those goals.

To be successful the Central American peace process cannot be based on promises alone. It must be based on credible standards of compliance, strict timetables for enforcement, and effective on-going means to verify both the democratic and security requirements of those agreements. We support the use of incentives and disincentives to achieve U.S. policy objectives.

We also endorse an open, consultative process with bipartisanship as the watchword for the development and success of a unified policy towards Central America. The Congress recognizes the need for consistency and continuity in policy and the responsibility of the Executive to administer and carry out that policy, the programs based upon it, and to conduct American diplomacy in the region. The Executive will consult regularly and report to the Congress on progress in meeting the goals of the peace and democratization process, including the use of assistance as outlined in this Accord.

Under Esquipulas II and the El Salvador Accord, insurgent forces are supposed to voluntarily reintegrate into their homeland under safe, democratic conditions. The United States shall encourage the Government of Nicaragua and the Nicaraguan Resistance to continue the cessation of hostilities currently in effect.

To implement our purposes, the Executive will propose and the bipartisan leadership of the Congress will act promptly after the Easter Recess to extend humanitarian assistance at current levels to the Resistance through February 28, 1990, noting that the Government of Nicaragua has agreed to hold new elections under international supervision just prior to that date. Those funds shall also be available to support voluntary reintegration or voluntary regional relocation by the Nicaraguan Resistance. Such voluntary reintegration or voluntary regional relocation assistance shall be provided in a manner supportive of the goals of the Central American nations, as expressed in the Esquipulas II agreement and the El Salvador Accord, including the goal of democratization within Nicaragua, and the reintegration plan to be developed pursuant to those accords.

We believe that democratization should continue throughout Central America in those nations in which it is not yet complete with progress towards strengthening of civilian leadership, the defense of human rights, the rule of law and functioning judicial systems, and consolidation of free, open, safe, political processes in which all groups and individuals can fairly compete for political leadership. We believe that democracy and peace in central America can create the conditions for economic integration and development that can benefit all the people of the region and pledge ourselves to examine new ideas to further those worthy goals.

While the Soviet Union and Cuba both publicly endorsed the Esquipulas Agreement, their continued aid and support of violence and subversion in Central America is in direct violation of that regional agreement. The United States believes that President Gorbachev's impending visit to Cuba represents an important opportunity for both the Soviet Union and Cuba to end all aid that supports subversion and destabilization in Central America as President Arias has requested and as the Central American peace process demands.

The United States Government retains ultimate responsibility to define its national interests and foreign policy, and nothing in this Accord shall be interpreted to infringe on that responsibility. The United States need not spell out in advance the nature or type of action that would be undertaken in response to threats to U.S. national security interests. Rather it should be sufficient to simply make clear that such threats will be met by any appropriate Constitutional means. The spirit of trust, bipartisanship, and common purpose expressed in this Accord between the Executive and the Congress shall continue to be the foundation for its full implementation and the achievement of democracy, security, and peace in Central America.

>George Bush
>>President of the United States
>James C. Wright, Jr.
>>Speaker of the House
>George J. Mitchell
>>Senate Majority Leader
>Thomas S. Foley
>>House Majority Leader
>Robert Dole
>>Senate Republican Leader
>Robert H. Michel
>>House Republican Leader

The White House
March 24, 1989

The Importance of Criticism

**Constructive Criticism of Foreign Policy
Is Essential to the Safety of the Nation; Remarks
by Senator Robert Taft, January 5, 1951 (Excerpt)[6]**

Mr. TAFT. Mr. President, I wish to thank the majority leader for his action in opening the floor of the Senate for debate before the President's State of the Union message. In view of the crisis in which we find ourselves today, the President may well take longer for the preparation of his message, but certainly that should not prevent discussion of vital national issues on the floor of the Senate.

During recent years a theory has developed that there shall be no criticism of the foreign policy of the administration, that any such criticism is an attack on the unity of the Nation, that it gives aid and comfort to the enemy, and that it sabotages any idea of a bipartisan foreign policy for the national benefit. I venture to state that this proposition is a fallacy and a very dangerous fallacy threatening the very existence of the Nation.

In very recent days we have heard appeals for unity from the administration and from its supporters. I suggest that these appeals are an attempt to cover up the past faults and failures of the administration and enable it to maintain the secrecy which has largely enveloped our foreign policy since the days of Franklin D. Roosevelt. It was a distinguished Democrat, President Woodrow Wilson, who denounced secret diplomacy and demanded open covenant openly arrived at. The administrations of President Roosevelt and President Truman have repudiated that wise democratic doctrine and assumed complete authority to make in secret the most vital decisions and commit this country to the most important and dangerous obligations.

As I see it, Members of Congress, and particularly Members of the Senate, have a constitutional obligation to reexamine constantly and discuss the foreign policy of the United States. If we permit appeals to unity to bring an end to that criticism, we endanger not only the constitutional liberties of the country, but even its future existence.

I may say that I hope the debate will occur on the floor of the Senate. I was invited to speak over the radio tonight following the speeches by former President Hoover and Mr. Dulles, and I declined because I felt that a statement of foreign policy by a Senator ought to be made on the floor of the Senate. I think there ought to be a continuous discussion of that policy during this session of the Senate.

Certainly when policies have been determined, unity in execution is highly desirable, and in the preparation for and the conduct of war it is essential. During recent months, the Republican minority has joined in granting to the President those powers which may be necessary to deal with the situation. We have not hesitated to pass a draft law, a law granting extensive powers of economic control, and almost unlimited appropriations for the Armed Forces. No action of the minority can be pointed to as in any way blocking or delaying the mobilization of our resources and our Armed Forces. If there has been any delay in the rearming, it has been in the administrative branch of the Government.

But it is part of our American system that basic elements of foreign policy shall be openly debated. It is said that such debate and the differences that may occur give aid and comfort to our possible enemies. I think that the value of such aid and comfort is grossly exaggerated. The only thing that can give real aid and comfort to the enemy is the adoption of a policy which plays into their hands as has our policy in the Far East. Such aid and comfort can only be prevented by frank criticism before such a policy is adopted.

Whatever the value of unity, it is also true that unity carried to unreasonable extremes can destroy a country. The Kaiser achieved unity in Germany. Hitler again achieved the same unity at the cost of freedom many years later. Mussolini achieved unity in Italy. The leaders of Japan through a method of so-called thought control achieved unity in Japan. In every case, policies adopted by these enforcers of unity led to the destruction of their own country. We have regarded ourselves as safe and a probable victor in every war. Today it is just as easy for us to adopt a false foreign policy leading to the destruction of our people as for any other nation to do so. The best safeguard against fatal error lies in continuous criticism and discussion to bring out the truth and develop the best program.

I have referred to the general tendency toward secrecy on the part of recent administrations. At Tehran and Yalta we secretly agreed to a zone of influence for Soviet Russia in Europe extending through the Baltic states and the Balkans and into the eastern zones of Austria and Germany. The result was to establish Russia in a position of power in central Europe extending through the Baltic states and the Balkans and into the eastern zones of Austria and Germany. The result was to establish Russia in a position of power in central Europe which today threatens the liberty of Western Europe and of the United States itself. Our leaders secretly agreed to turn over control of Manchuria to Russia, and later hampered the operations of the Nationalist Government in combat against the Communists without consultation of any kind with Congress. In Germany our leaders adopted the Morgenthau plan while constantly denying that they were doing anything of the kind, and without submitting the questions in any way to Congress for discussion. The President without authority, as I pointed out in my speech on June 28, 1950, committed American troops to Korea without any consultation whatever with Congress and, in my opinion, without authority of law. He did not even tell Congress there was a war for 2 weeks after we were engaged. The President claims the right without consultation with Congress to decide whether or not we should use the atomic bomb.

We see now the beginning of an agreement to send a specified number of American troops to Europe without that question ever having been discussed in the Congress of the United States. The Atlantic Pact may have committed us to send arms to the other members of the pact, but no one ever maintained that it committed us to send many American troops to Europe.

A new policy is being formulated without consulting the Congress or the people.

In other cases policies have been developed to a point where the honor of this country is committed before any serious debate by the public is permitted. Thus in the case of the Marshall plan and the Atlantic Pact, the programs were broached in the most general terms, then substantially advanced by the State Department through secret briefing conferences with many friendly groups and thorough indoctrination of friendly editors, columnists and commentators before they were submitted to the public or to Congress. After that if anyone dared to suggest criticisms or even a thorough debate, he was at once branded as an isolationist and a saboteur of unity and the bipartisan foreign policy.

More and more it has become customary to make agreements instead of treaties thus bypassing the power intended to be conferred on the Senate to pass on the wisdom of important principles of foreign policy. It is still fashionable to meet any criticism by cries of isolationism just as Mr. Hoover's recent speech has been treated. Criticisms are met by the calling of names rather than by intelligent debate.

I do not intend to say that a bipartisan foreign policy could not be adopted, but there has been no real bipartisan policy, at any rate since the 1948 election. It is a proper ideal and the minority will always be ready to answer any appeal for advice and cooperation. Only there cannot be a bipartisan foreign policy unless it is a policy on which both parties agree, and it is unlikely that there can be such agreement unless the administration is more inclined to give consideration to the views of the minority and to modify its own views than it has done in recent months. We certainly would be prepared to make concessions, but certainly the concessions should not be a one-way street. I quite realize the difficulty of any President in consulting the minority in advance on every question of foreign policy, and I do not blame him for his failure to urge or adopt a bipartisan policy. But certainly the Republican minority cannot be attacked for failure to agree on policies on which they have not even been consulted or on policies which they may regard as detrimental to the welfare of the Nation.

The result of a general practice of secrecy in all the initial steps of foreign policy has been to deprive the Senate and Congress of the substance of the powers conferred on them by the Constitution.

We would be lacking in the fulfillment of our obligations and false to our oaths if we did not criticize policies which may lead to unnecessary war, policies which may wreck the internal economy of this country and vastly weaken our economic abilities through unsound taxation or inflation, policies which may commit us to obligations we are utterly unable to perform, and thus discredit us in the eyes of the world. Criticism and debate are essential if we are to maintain the constitutional liberties of this country and its democratic heritage. Under the present administration, at any rate, criticism and debate I think are essential to avoid danger and possible destruction of our Nation....

Southeast Asia Resolution; Dissenting Remarks
by Senator Wayne Morse, August 6, 1954 (Excerpts)[7]

Mr. MORSE. Mr. President, I rise to speak in opposition to the joint resolution. I do so with a very sad heart. But I consider the resolution, as I considered the resolution of 1955, known as the Formosa resolution, and the subsequent resolution, known as the Middle East resolution, to be naught but a resolution which embodies a predated declaration of war.

Article I, section 8 of our Constitution does not permit the President to make war at his discretion. Therefore I stand on this issue as I have stood before in the Senate, perfectly willing to take the judgment of history as to the merits of my cause. I note in passing that the warnings which the Senator from New York, Mr. Lehman, and the senior Senator from Oregon uttered in 1955 in opposition to the Formosa Resolution have been proved to be correct by history. I am satisfied that history will render a final verdict in opposition to the joint resolution introduced today....

I yield to no other Senator, or to anyone else in this country in my opposition to communism and all that communism stands for.

In our time a great struggle, which may very well be a deathlock struggle, is going on in the world between freedom on the one hand and the totalitarianism of communism on the other.

However, I am satisfied that that struggle can never be settled by war. I am satisfied that if the hope of anyone is that the struggle between freedom and communism can be settled by war, and that course is followed, both freedom and communism will lose, for there will be no victory in that war.

Because of our own deep interest in the struggle against communism, we in the United States are inclined to overlook some of the other struggles which are occupying others. We try to force every issue into the context of freedom versus communism. That is one of our great mistakes in Asia. There is much communism there, and much totalitarianism in other forms. We say we are opposing communism there, but that does not mean we are advancing freedom, because we are not.

Senators will note as I proceed in the presentation of my case in opposition to the resolution that I believe the only hope for the establishment of a permanent peace in the world is to practice our oft-repeated American professing that we believe in the substitution of the rule of law for the jungle law of military force as a means of settling disputes which threaten the peace of the world.

The difficulty with that professing or preaching by the United States is that the United States, like some Communist nations, does not practice it.

I wish to make one last introductory remark in the hope that more will understand the message of this speech, although we sometimes deplore the possibility of understanding on a subject matter that stirs so much emotion, so much feeling, and so much passion in the minds of so-called superpatriots, who seem to feel that if one raises any question or expresses any criticism of the policies of our country in the field of foreign policy, one's very patriotism is subject to question....

My foreign policy philosophy is based on a great teaching of a great teacher in this body, one who undoubtedly exercised more influence on me in the field of foreign policy that any other person; a great Republican, who became chairman of the Committee on Foreign Relations; who was one of the architects of the San Francisco Charter; who joined with Franklin Delano Roosevelt in the announcement of that great statement in the field of foreign policy, that politics should stop at the water's edge. I refer, of course, to the incomparable Arthur Vandenberg, of Michigan.

Senators within my hearing have heard me say before that I was deeply moved by that dramatic account of Arthur Vandenberg, in which he told, so many times, how he ceased being the leading isolationist in the Senate and became the leading internationalist. It was before the atomic bomb was finally perfected, but after it was known that the atomic bomb would be successful in its perfection.

Franklin Roosevelt called to the White House late one night the leaders of Congress, the leading scientists of the country, who were working on the bomb at that time, and the military leaders of our Defense Establishment who were still stationed in Washington. As Arthur Vandenberg used to say, "We were briefed, and the conference continued until the wee hours of the morning. The scientists convinced all that there was no question that the bomb would work. Then the discussion turned to the implications of this great discovery of science."

Senator Vandenberg used to say to us, "When I came out of the White House in the wee hours of that morning, I knew that while I had been in there that night, the world had so shrunken that there no longer was any place in American politics for an isolationist."

It was then that the great record of internationalism was begun to be made by the incomparable Vandenberg. I paraphrase him, but accurately, for my speech today rests upon this tenet, this unanswerable teaching of Vandenberg....

That tenet of Vandenberg's is as follows: There is no hope for permanent peace in the world until all the nations--not merely some, not merely those we like, not merely those we think are friendly--but until all the nations are willing to establish a system of international justice through law, to the procedures of which will be submitted each and every international dispute that threatens the peace of the world, anywhere in the world, for final and binding determination, to be enforced by an international organization, such as the United Nations....

Vandenberg left us this great ideal. It will take years to implement it. But we must always move forward, not backward. We are moving in Asia today, but the movement of the United States in Asia is not in the direction of Vandenberg's principle.

It makes no difference who says that our objective is peace, even if he be the President of the United States. Our actions speak louder than words; and our actions in Asia today are the actions of warmaking.

As I speak on the floor of the Senate at this moment, the United States is making war in Asia.

I shall never give up, short of the actual passage of a declaration of war, my prayerful hope for peace and my prayerful hope that we will substitute the ideal of the rule of law through the only international organization that exists and that has any hope, in my judgment, of applying the rule--the United Nations.

Thus I say that the incident that has inspired the joint resolution we have just heard read is as much the doing of the United States as it is the doing of North Vietnam....

Likewise, there are many congressional politicians who would evade their responsibilities as to American foreign policy in Asia by use of the specious argument that "foreign policy is a matter for the executive branch of the Government. That branch has information no Congressman has access to." Of course, such an alibi for evading congressional responsibility in the field of foreign policy may be based on lack of understanding, or a convenient forgetting of our system of checks and balances that exists and should be exercised in the relationships between and among our three coordinate and coequal branches of government.

Granted that there are many in Congress who would prefer to pass the buck to the White House, the State Department, and the Pentagon Building in respect to our unilateral American military action in Asia. And this resolution gives them the vehicle. Nevertheless, I am satisfied that once the American people come to understand the facts involved in the ill-fated military operations in Asia, they will hold to an accounting those Members of Congress who abdicate their responsibilities in the field of foreign policy....

The United States has much to lose and little to gain by continuing our unilateral military action in southeast Asia, unsanctioned by the United Nations and unaccompanied by allies.

No nation in history has had such a great opportunity as this one now has to strike a blow for peace at an international conference table.

I shall not support any substitute which takes the form of a predated declaration of war. In my judgment, that is what the pending joint resolution is.

I shall not support any delegation of the duty of Congress--of Congress, not the President--to determine an issue of war or peace.

I shall not support any substitute which takes the form of military action to expand the war or that encourages our puppets in Saigon to expand the war.

Adherence to the United Nations Charter is the only policy that affords the hope of leading the American people out of this jam without a war. I shall continue to plead for such a policy as long as time remains.

If war overtakes us first, then we will have not choice but to unite behind its prosecution.

But, first, that calls for a declaration of war and not a resolution that seeks to authorize the President to make war without our declaring war. That was the position I took in 1955; and I incorporate by reference every argument I used in opposition to a preventive war resolution of that date.

But I see no more chance of conventional military victory in North Vietnam and China than in South Vietnam, and I therefore plead that the SEATO treaty and the United Nations Charter, rather than solitary force of arms, guide our actions in southeast Asia.

I am convinced that a continuation of the U.S. unilateral military action in southeast Asia, which has now taken on the aspects of open aggressive fighting, endangers the peace of the world....

The Dominican Republic; Comments by
Senator William Fulbright, October 22, 1965 (Excerpts)[8]

Mr. FULBRIGHT. Mr. President, I have followed with interest the comments made by my colleagues, by the press, and by private individuals after my speech of September 15 regarding the Dominican Republic. I have also followed with interest events in the other body that may have been related to my speech.

Much of the discussion, I have noted to my surprise, has been about me rather than about the Dominican Republic and Latin America. Some of these personal comments have been complimentary, and to those who made them I express my thanks. Others have been uncomplimentary, and to those who made them I can only say that our country is still strong enough to survive an occasional dissenting view even though the consensus is virtually unanimous.

There has been a good deal of discussion as to whether it is proper for the chairman of the Senate Foreign Relations Committee to make a speech critical of an administration of his own party which he generally supports. There is something to be said on both sides of this question and it is certainly one which I considered with care before deciding to make my speech on the Dominican Republic. I concluded, after hearing the testimony of administration witnesses in the Committee on Foreign Relations, that I could do more to encourage carefully considered policies in the future by initiating a public discussion than by acquiescing silently in a policy I believed to be mistaken. It seemed to me, therefore, that, despite any controversy and annoyance to individuals, I was performing a service to the administration by stating my views publicly.

I do not like taking a public position criticizing a Democratic administration which in most respects I strongly support; I do not like it at all. Neither do I like being told, as I have been told, that my statement was "irresponsible" or that it has given aid and comfort to the enemies of the United States. I am quite prepared to examine evidence suggesting that my statement contained errors of fact or judgment; I am not prepared to accept the charge that a statement following upon many hours of listening to testimony in the Foreign Relations Committee and many more hours of examining and evaluating relevant documents was irresponsible. Nor do I take kindly to the charge that I gave aid and comfort to the enemies of the United States. If that accusation is to be pressed--and I should hope it would not be--an interesting discussion could be developed as to whether it is my criticisms of U.S. policy in the Dominican Republic or the policy itself which has given aid and comfort to our enemies.

A Senator has a duty to support his President and his party, but he also has a duty to express his views on major issues. In the case of the Dominican crisis I felt that, however reluctant I might be to criticize the administration--and I was very reluctant--it was nonetheless my responsibility to do so, for two principal reasons.

First. I believe that the chairman of the Committee on Foreign Relations has a special obligation to offer the best advice he can on matters of foreign policy; it is an obligation, I believe, which is inherent in the chairmanship, which takes precedence over party loyalty, and which has nothing to do with whether the chairman's views are solicited or desired by people in the executive branch.

Second. I thought it my responsibility to comment on U.S. policy in the Dominican Republic because the political opposition, whose function it is to criticize, was simply not doing so. It did not because it obviously approved of U.S. intervention in the Dominican Republic and presumably, had it been in office, would have done the same thing. The result of this peculiar situation was that a highly controversial policy was being carried out without controversy--without debate, without review, without that necessary calling to account which is a vital part of the democratic process. Again and again, in the weeks following the committee hearing I noted the absence of any challenge to statements appearing in the press and elsewhere which clearly contradicted evidence available to the Committee on Foreign Relations.

Under these circumstances I am not impressed with suggestions that I had no right to speak as I did on Santo Domingo.

The real question, it seems to me, is whether I had the right not to speak.

Insofar as it represents a genuine reconciliation of differences, a consensus is a fine thing; insofar as it represents the concealment of differences, it is a miscarriage of democratic procedure. I think we Americans tend to put too high a value on unanimity--on bipartisanship in foreign policy, on politics stopping at the water's edge, on turning a single face to the world--as if there were something dangerous and illegitimate about honest differences of opinion honestly expressed by honest men. Probably because we have been united about so many things for so long, including the basic values of our free society, we tend to be mistrustful of intellectual dissent, confusing it with personal hostility and political loyalty....

Far from being the danger many of us make it out to be, responsible dissent is one of the great strengths of democracy. France, for example, is unquestionably in a stronger position today in her relations with the emerging nations of Asia and Africa because during the years of her colonial wars in Indochina and Algeria a large and articulate minority refused to acquiesce in what was being done and, by speaking out, pointed the way to the enlightened policies of the Fifth Republic. The British Labor Party, to take another example, not only protested the Suez invasion in 1956 but did so while the invasion was being carried out; by so doing, the opposition performed the patriotic service of helping Britain to recover its good name in the wake of a disastrous adventure, starting to repair the damage while the damage was still being done.

It seems to me a manifestation of the tyranny of the majority that there has been so much talk about when it is proper for a Senator to make a speech and so little about the subject matter involved, which was the Dominican Republic and Latin America. It was my intention on September 15 to start a discussion about these and not about myself. There is a very great deal to be said about U.S. policy in Latin America--about political and economic reform and the Alliance for Progress, about collective security and the Organization of American States, about social revolutions and the interests of the United States. I should like very much to hear the views of my colleagues on these and other matters, including the suggestion tentatively put forth in my statement of September 15 that an inter-American partnership of equals in the long run might be advanced by a loosening of ties in the short run....

Notes

1. U.S. Congress. Senate. 79th Congress, 1st session. Executive Report No. 8.
2. U.S. Congress. Senate. 80th Congress, 2d session. Report No. 935.
3. U.S. Congress. Senate. 81st Congress, 1st session. Executive Report No. 8.
4. U.S. Congress. Senate. 82d Congress, 2d session. Executive Report No. 2.
5. U.S. Office of Federal Register. National Archives and Record Administration. Weekly Compilation of Presidential Documents. Vol. 25, no. 12, p. 420-421.
6. Congressional Record, Vol. 97, part 1, January 5, 1951, p. 55-61.
7. Congressional Record, Vol. 110, part 14, August 6, 1964, p. 18133-9.
8. Congressional Record, Vol. 111, part 21, October 22, 1965, p. 28372-9.

PART THREE

Strengthening Executive-Legislative Consultation on Foreign Policy

(House Foreign Affairs Committee Print, October 1983)

FOREIGN AFFAIRS COMMITTEE PRINT

CONGRESS AND FOREIGN POLICY SERIES

No. 8

Strengthening Executive-Legislative Consultation on Foreign Policy

OCTOBER 1983

U.S. GOVERNMENT PRINTING OFFICE
WASHINGTON : 1983

COMMITTEE ON FOREIGN AFFAIRS

CLEMENT J. ZABLOCKI, Wisconsin, *Chairman*

DANTE B. FASCELL, Florida
LEE H. HAMILTON, Indiana
GUS YATRON, Pennsylvania
STEPHEN J. SOLARZ, New York
DON BONKER, Washington
GERRY E. STUDDS, Massachusetts
ANDY IRELAND, Florida
DAN MICA, Florida
MICHAEL D. BARNES, Maryland
HOWARD WOLPE, Michigan
GEO. W. CROCKETT, JR., Michigan
SAM GEJDENSON, Connecticut
MERVYN M. DYMALLY, California
TOM LANTOS, California
PETER H. KOSTMAYER, Pennsylvania
ROBERT G. TORRICELLI, New Jersey
LAWRENCE J. SMITH, Florida
HOWARD L. BERMAN, California
HARRY M. REID, Nevada
MEL LEVINE, California
EDWARD F. FEIGHAN, Ohio
TED WEISS, New York
ROBERT GARCIA, New York

WILLIAM S. BROOMFIELD, Michigan
LARRY WINN, JR., Kansas
BENJAMIN A. GILMAN, New York
ROBERT J. LAGOMARSINO, California
JOEL PRITCHARD, Washington
JIM LEACH, Iowa
TOBY ROTH, Wisconsin
OLYMPIA J. SNOWE, Maine
HENRY J. HYDE, Illinois
GERALD B. H. SOLOMON, New York
DOUGLAS K. BEREUTER, Nebraska
MARK D. SILJANDER, Michigan
ED ZSCHAU, California

JOHN J. BRADY, Jr., *Chief of Staff*
MARGARET GOODMAN, *Staff Consultant*
ROXANNE PERUGINO, *Staff Assistant*

SUBCOMMITTEE ON EUROPE AND THE MIDDLE EAST

LEE H. HAMILTON, Indiana, *Chairman*

TOM LANTOS, California
ANDY IRELAND, Florida
MERVYN M. DYMALLY, California
ROBERT G. TORRICELLI, New Jersey
LAWRENCE J. SMITH, Florida
MEL LEVINE, California

LARRY WINN, JR., Kansas
MARK D. SILJANDER, Michigan
ED ZSCHAU, California

MICHAEL H. VAN DUSEN, *Staff Director*
ALISON BRENNER FORTIER, *Minority Staff Consultant*
KENNETH B. MOSS, *Subcommittee Staff Consultant*
JOHN E. HARE, *Subcommittee Staff Consultant*

FOREWORD

This report on strengthening executive-legislative consultation in foreign policy is the eighth and final volume of a series on congressional-executive relations in foreign policymaking prepared by the Congressional Research Service for the House Committee on Foreign Affairs.

The need for improved congressional-executive relations in foreign policy is an issue of continuing concern among many members of the House Foreign Affairs Committee. From 1972 to 1975, the committee supported the formation of, and participation in, the work of the Commission on the Organization of the Government for the Conduct of Foreign Policy. In 1977, the committee's Special Subcommittee on Investigations, chaired by Representative Lee H. Hamilton, conducted a series of hearings and issued a report entitled "Congress and Foreign Policy." Subsequently, the Foreign Affairs and National Defense Division of the Congressional Research Service was requested to review the report's recommendations for improving the quality and nature of congressional input into foreign policy, and to consider alternate methods of implementing the recommendations.

In response to the request, a series of functional and case studies, based on extensive interviews and roundtable workshops, were undertaken. This concluding volume analyzes the findings of the series.

Issues concerning the effectiveness of the consultation process as it impacts on foreign policy have assumed additional importance since the Supreme Court decision in June 1983 declared the congressional veto unconstitutional. In view of the number of congressional veto provisions in foreign policy legislation, this volume includes as appendixes a review of the potential impact of the Supreme Court decision on the legislative-executive balance in foreign policy, a list of legislative veto provisions in foreign policy legislation and a study of the effect of the Supreme Court decision on legislation dealing with arms sales and transfers, which was the subject of volume 7 in this series. These three studies were prepared by the Congressional Research Service.

This volume also includes appendixes summarizing the recommendations of the Murphy Commission on the Organization of the Government for the Conduct of Foreign Policy, and of the Hamilton subcommittee's 1977 report "Congress and Foreign Policy," and an annotated bibliography of readings on executive-congressional relations in foreign policy.

This report "Strengthening Executive-Legislative Consultation on Foreign Policy" was prepared by Ellen C. Collier, Specialist in U.S.

Foreign Policy at the Congressional Research Service. The findings and observations contained in this report are those of the author and do not necessarily represent the views of the Committees on Foreign Affairs or its members.

CLEMENT J. ZABLOCKI,
Chairman, Committee on Foreign Affairs.
LEE H. HAMILTON,
Chairman, Subcommittee on Europe and the Middle East.

PREFACE

"From a legislative viewpoint, the crux of the problem between the executive branch and the Congress in foreign policy today is the inadequate state of consultation between the two branches."[1] This was a chief conclusion of the House Foreign Affairs Special Subcommittee on Investigations, under the chairmanship of Representative Lee H. Hamilton, following extensive hearings on the role of Congress in foreign policy. Subsequently Chairman Clement J. Zablocki of the Foreign Affairs Committee and Representative Hamilton, now chairman of the Subcommittee on Europe and the Middle East, asked the Congressional Research Service to study foreign policy consultation between the two branches and methods to improve it.

In response, the Foreign Affairs and National Defense Division of the Congressional Research Service has been conducting a special study on problems of legislative-executive consultation in foreign policy. A series of case studies, summarized in part 2 of this report, examined the communication between the two branches on specific foreign policy decisions in order to gain increased understanding of the processes involved.[2] These were supplemented by analyses of the role of Congress in specific cases in the annual publication "Congress and Foreign Policy" which has been prepared for the House Foreign Affairs Committee since 1974,[3] and by cases which may be found in the bibliography in appendix C.

A series of functional studies, summarized in chapter VI, analyzed the feasibility of alternative methods of implementing recommendations that had been made by the Hamilton committee. Two of these studies explored problems in the executive and legislative branches affecting consultation and a third concentrated on methods of improving foreign policy information for Congress.[4]

---

[1] U.S. Congress. Committee on International Relations. Special Subcommittee on Investigations. Congress and Foreign Policy. Report. Washington, U.S. Government Printing Office, 1977, p. 2. Hereafter referred to as Special Subcommittee on Investigations. Congress and Foreign Policy. Report.

[2] U.S. Congress. House. Committee on Foreign Affairs. Committee prints in the Congress and Foreign Policy Series. Washington, U.S. Government Printing Office, 1979–1982:
No. 1. Executive-Legislative Consultation on China Policy, 1978–79. By Robert G. Sutter. June 1980. 42 pp.
No. 3. Congressional-Executive Relations and the Turkish Arms Embargo. By Ellen B. Laipson. June 1981. 60 pp.
No. 6. Executive-Legislative Consultation on Foreign Policy; Sanctions against Rhodesia. By Raymond W. Copson. September 1982. 69 pp. Hereafter referred to as Sanctions against Rhodesia.
No. 7. Executive-Legislative Consultation on U.S. Arms Sales. By Richard F. Grimmett. December 1982. 39 pp.

[3] U.S. Congress. Committee on Foreign Affairs. Congress and Foreign Policy. [annual volume]. Washington, U.S. Government Printing Office.

[4] U.S. Congress. House. Committee on Foreign Affairs. Committee prints in the Congress and Foreign Policy Series. Washington, U.S. Government Printing Office, 1979–1982:
No. 2. Executive-Legislative Consultation on Foreign Policy: Strengthening Executive Branch Procedures. By Joseph T. Kendrick. May 1981. 77 pp.
No. 4. Executive-Legislative Consultation on Foreign Policy: Strengthening Foreign Policy Information Sources for Congress. By Sam Postbrief. February 1982. 84 pp.
No. 5. Executive-Legislative Consultation on Foreign Policy: Strengthening the Legislative Side. By Ellen C. Collier. April 1982. 85 pp.

The project also reviewed all the recommendations made by the Hamilton subcommittee in its report of 1977 and the relevant recommendations made by the Commission on the Organization of the Government for the Conduct of Foreign Policy, or the Murphy Commission, in its report of June 1975. A status report on their recommendations is included as appendix B.

In order to understand the perceptions of persons actually involved in consultation, the Congressional Research Service held a number of workshops and seminars to discuss the subject. In addition, members of the project interviewed more than 200 persons in both branches concerned with making foreign policy, including Members of Congress representing both political parties, congressional staff, and administration officials of all levels.

The author gratefully acknowledges the assistance of all those who gave their time and energy to participate in the interviews and workshops, which were conducted on a not-for-attribution basis, and to those who reviewed some or all of the manuscript. She is particularly indebted to the authors of the studies in the series on which this analysis is based: Robert G. Sutter, Joseph T. Kendrick, Ellen B. Laipson, Sam Postbrief, Raymond W. Copson, and Richard F. Grimmett. Janice L. Carter prepared the annotated bibliography, and Robert Lockwood, Jonathan Sanford, Theodor W. Galdi, Marjorie Ann Browne, and K. Larry Storrs provided additional research. James W. Robinson, Coordinator of Review for the Congressional Research Service, made many helpful suggestions.

Finally, the author would like to express her thanks to Stanley Heginbotham, Chief of the Foreign Affairs and National Defense Division, who provided guidance and support and carefully reviewed all the studies, and to Margaret Goodman, staff consultant of the House Foreign Affairs Committee, and Michael Van Dusen, staff director of the Subcommittee on Europe and the Middle East, who also gave continuing support and helpful criticisms and ideas throughout the project.

PRINCIPAL FINDINGS

A. THE MEANING OF EFFECTIVE CONSULTATION

Effective consultation requires meaningful and timely involvement of an appropriate range of Members of Congress in the making of significant foreign policy decisions by the executive branch. Consultation could be greatly improved even if it was not ideal in every aspect. Four components determine its adequacy and effectiveness:

Range of Members consulted.—The executive branch can get varying and valuable insights by consulting the leadership, relevant committees and subcommittees, and individual Members who are particularly interested in an issue. The range may be smaller but still effective, however, if it portrays the views and concerns of enough of the Congress to help design a policy that can win the necessary support.

Timing.—If congressional insights and guidance are to be fruitful, the executive branch should consult Congress early in policy formation, at least as soon as the options have been identified but before a decision has been made. The timing may be effective, however, if there is still room for modification of a policy to take into account congressional views.

Significance of the issues.—To prevent embarrassments, the executive branch would do well to consult the Senate on any significant treaty or nomination and the Congress on any issue which may require legislation, appropriations, or other congressional action. Nevertheless, consultation may be effective as long as it includes policies that involve a major commitment of funds or potential commitment of armed forces, or that may require sustained national support.

Attitudes.—At best, both the President and Congress would enter consultations in a cooperative spirit, seeking the best policy outcome for the country. Consultation may be effective, however, if each side acknowledges the legitimate role of the other and has an understanding of the other branch and the international and domestic factors shaping its decisions.

B. THE RECORD OF CONSULTATION

The executive branch seldom consults effectively with Congress on foreign policy despite a great deal of communication between the branches. Most of the communication is simply the transmission of information that has been requested by Congress or the advocacy of a course of action that the executive branch has already determined.

When appropriations or legislation is needed, as in the case of foreign aid, the executive branch may bargain with Congress to get what it wants. Sometimes legislation mandates consultation, as in the

Trade Agreements Act of 1979. But on most important decisions, if the President has full control of the tools for action, he takes action without consulting Congress. Almost every postwar President has made decisions to use U.S. Armed Forces without consulting Congress in advance, but instead, informing them after the decision.

In the cases examined for this study, good consultation was found only in the Marshall plan. In crises and the most crucial decisions examined here—the intervention in the Dominican Republic and the timing of the establishment of diplomatic relations with China—Congress was informed after the fact. Only on the cases where legislation was involved—the Turkish arms embargo, an amendment affecting observance of the United Nations sanctions on Rhodesian chrome, arms sales, the drafting of the Taiwan Relations Act—was there substantial negotiation that might qualify as a type of consultation. Even these cases did not constitute effective consultation. The negotiations were usually a response to clear indications that Members of Congress might not "go along" with the position of the executive branch; they started after the position of the executive branch was so set that only marginal changes could be made; and they were done in such a way that mistrust between the branches increased.

C. Why Consult? The Potentialities

Consultation offers a way for the two branches to work together in formulating foreign policy within the constitutional separation of powers. Unless some system to achieve this purpose is developed, the alternatives are for one branch to recede from its foreign policy position, continued confrontation, or some type of change in the basic constitutional system.

Judicious consultation—not only with Congress but often with other domestic or foreign leaders—is usually a part of good policymaking. It indicates that enough time has been taken in shaping a policy to seek the views of those whose support is required for the policy to be successful. It also indicates a willingness to have the policy exposed to criticism, debate, and suggestions for improvement. Often it focuses debate on the substance of the problem and clarifies the issues and areas of agreement and disagreement.

Consultation could be a valuable tool for both the legislative and executive branches. It could be useful to the executive branch as a consensus-building device to increase the likelihood of having the congressional and public support necessary to carry out a policy or program. It could be useful to the Congress as a channel for constructively influencing foreign policy. These potential benefits appear fairly clear, yet good consultation is and has always been quite rare. The reasons for this apparent contradiction are, however, rather formidable and a matter of primary concern.

D. What to Expect of Consultation: The Limitations

While consultation can help, neither the executive branch nor Congress should expect consultation to end all differences between the two branches. The executive branch cannot expect consultation to guarantee legislative support, and Members of Congress cannot expect that their advice is always taken.

For the administration, the risk remains that wider dissemination of knowledge about a proposed policy may lead to public discussion of matters that some might prefer to be kept secret, or that it may give opponents time and information with which to mobilize. Members of Congress take a risk that they may have to take a public position on a matter they would prefer not to and that they will have to share in the responsibility if policy decisions prove unwise.

Differences of opinion on consultation are not easily resolved by resort to empirical analysis. It is possible to show, as this study series does, that in retrospect, specific national foreign policy performances could have been much improved by effective consultation; but it is also possible for skeptics to argue that as a practical matter a major effort at consultation over the years would have led to more confusing and erratic leadership, more decisional paralysis, and a generally poorer national performance in foreign and security affairs. A record of minimal consultation in foreign policy exists for analysis and evaluation. No comparable long-term experience with a mutually forthcoming consultative posture exists for examination.

E. Barriers to Consultation

There are seven parallel problems in the executive branch and in Congress that impede consultation. All are basic, more or less permanent, and are central to any effort to improve consultation.

1. NEGATIVE ATTITUDES

In both banches, there are persistent attitudes that discourage consultation. Most executive branch officials do not want to consult with Congress, taking the view that Congress has no place "meddling" in foreign policy or that Members of Congress are too parochial in viewpoint and have nothing to contribute to foreign policy. Some Members of Congress are willing to leave foreign policymaking to the executive branch. Others are suspicious and distrustful of executive branch officials and concerned that consultation may lead to cooptation and prevent proper criticism of the executive branch by Congress.

2. DIFFERING POLITICAL OBJECTIVES AND INSTITUTIONAL NEEDS

Each branch has its own problems, objectives, and methods for career advancement. Foreign Service officers and executive officials making foreign policy work primarily in the worlds of diplomacy and bureaucracy. Members of Congress work primarily in the world of Capitol Hill and their constituencies. Both make selective use of the press. Each world has its own values, and sometimes the values conflict; for example, diplomats find secrecy and subtleness helpful in negotiations while Members of Congress value publicity and openness with the American people.

Both branches meet in the political arena, and it is there that issues are ultimately decided according to votes in Congress or Presidential and congressional elections. The political arena provides some alliances and mutual understanding between the branches, but it also often adds to mistrust, despite a greater tradition of bipartisanship in foreign policy than in domestic questions.

The executive branch prefers minimal consultation that allows officials flexibility and freedom of action, partly because this mode of operation usually works. In several decades of foreign policy, there have been relatively few major embarrassments or confrontations, and there is little proof that those would have been avoided by more extensive consultation. Many in Congress, on the other hand, view improved consultation as a means to a larger and more effective role in a strengthened foreign policy.

3. LACK OF KNOWLEDGE AND UNDERSTANDING OF THE OTHER BRANCH

The barrier created by differing institutional interests is heightened by the lack of knowledge of one branch by the other. Executive branch officials handling foreign policy, who have a high rate of turnover, often estimate opinion in Congress incorrectly, or lack the skills of many private lobbyists in knowing who in Congress holds power in a particular instance. Similarly, Members of Congress often appear insensitive to executive branch concern for the complexities of multiparty negotiations, the feelings of foreign officials, or diplomatic efforts to press quietly on a delicate matter.

4. PERSONALITY PROBLEMS

Effective consultation has sometimes been impeded by persons with recessive, abrasive or arrogant personalities, just as it has been enhanced by persons adept in the skills involved.

5. PRESSURE OF TIME

Time is a factor inhibiting consultation, not usually because of the urgency of the problems but because executive officials and Members of Congress alike are busy people. Executive officials often do not take time for consultation with the congressional side until a vote on relevant legislation appears to be in danger.

6. STRUCTURAL PROBLEMS

The diffusion of power within both branches makes it difficult for each to reach internal agreement and results in multiple lines of communication between the branches. Often several executive agencies and congressional committees are involved in an issue. The President can ultimately resolve disputes among agencies and speak for the executive branch, but there is no similar central power or spokesperson for Congress. In addition, it is more difficult to develop any policy that can be said to be the "congressional" position on an issue because of the differences inherent among 535 independent Members and the jurisdictional and other rivalries among Members, subcommittees, committees, and the Senate and House. Only a formal vote can determine a congressional position.

7. INTEREST GROUPS

Interest groups may be a barrier to effective consultation when they add to mistrust between the branches, although they may also be a channel of communication and provide timely, frankly advocative information.

F. STEPS THE EXECUTIVE BRANCH CAN TAKE TO IMPROVE CONSULTATION

The executive branch could consult more effectively by working on any of the four components to:
—Increase the range of Members consulted;
—Consult earlier, while there is still time for modification of a policy to meet congressional views;
—Consult with a more receptive attitude, recognizing the legitimacy of the congressional role in foreign policy and its contribution and problems;
—Focus consultation efforts on the most significant issues.

Three types of measures offer means to improve executive branch consultative performance:

1. Policy guidelines.—Directives from the President or Secretary of State could encourage consultation, suggest a program of consultation that could be varied according to the importance of the issue, and pinpoint responsibility for identifying priority issues for consultation and following through.

2. Confidence-building measures.—Programs to build trust and confidence between the two branches could include additional personnel exchange programs, a permanent office on Capitol Hill for congressional liaison officers to expedite constituent services, and making available Foreign Service officers to discuss issues with Members of Congress and staff on request.

3. Training, awareness, and information programs.—The Department of State could increase its knowledge and understanding about Congress by wider dissemination of literature on Congress including the Congressional Record, better tracking of views of Members and committees, and more extensive inclusion of material on Congress in Foreign Service Institute courses.

An executive branch system to improve consultation need not be elaborate. The congressional desire for consultation is by no means insatiable, contrary to President Carter's complaint.[1] This survey indicates that the executive branch could go far toward satisfying the congressional desire for consultation simply by meeting with appropriate congressional groups prior to taking major foreign policy actions. Many in Congress seek recognition of their role in foreign policy decisions and the opportunity to be heard in the making of foreign policy. A large number are prepared to accept the fact that their perceptions and concerns may influence decisions only on the margin or perhaps not at all.

---

[1] "It seemed that Congress had an insatiable desire for consultation, which, despite all our efforts, we were never able to meet. It was not for lack of trying." Carter, Jimmy. Keeping Faith: Memories of a President. New York, Bantam Books, 1982, p. 71.

Members of Congress complain primarily when the executive branch takes an important action without discussion with any congressional representatives, even the leadership. They have seldom complained if the executive branch made a bona fide attempt to consult the leadership or appropriate committees. Even when only a few leaders were informed about an action and many felt the consultation had not been adequate, as in the case of the Zaire airlift, criticism has been much restrained.

Similarly, Members have seldom complained about nonconsultation on unimportant matters. They have shown the most concern about lack of consultation on actions that might involve U.S. Armed Forces in hostilities—the incursions into Cambodia in May 1970, the assistance to Angolan forces in 1975, the attempt to rescue the hostages from Iran in 1980—or sudden actions with far-reaching implications for U.S. foreign policy, such as the announcement at the end of 1978 of diplomatic relations with China and the termination of the defense treaty with Taiwan.

G. Steps Congress Can Take to Improve Consultation

Improvement of consultation depends as much on the actions of Congress as of the executive branch. Congress can strengthen the components of effective consultation by designating whom to consult, initiatives to bring about early consultation, providing incentives to consult on priority issues, and demonstrating greater understanding of diplomatic problems.

Four approaches offer means for Congress to promote systematically effective consultation:

1. *Legislation to improve information mechanisms.*—Provisions requiring consultation or reports could be tightened by specifying the Members or committees of Congress to be involved, establishing a deadline, filling in gaps in the requirements, and utilizing the information received more fully.

2. *Increasing leverage.*—The best incentive for consultation has proved to be congressional power to prevent the executive branch from taking actions not authorized or approved by Congress. With the legislative veto declared unconstitutional in the *Chadha* case, Congress is faced with a decision of whether to withdraw authorizations which permit wide Presidential latitude or to seek new arrangements assuring a congressional voice in policies.

3. *More effective consultative meetings.*—Clearly designated consultative meetings of subcommittees and committees with executive officials could focus on options rather than on acquiring information. After a policy is determined, they could focus on oversight and problems being encountered in carrying out a policy.

4. *Initiatives in pursuing information and proposing solutions.*—The introduction of legislation proposing policies and programs has been an effective way to get the executive branch to listen to Congress. Travel abroad has proved helpful in providing new information and increasing congressional understanding of foreign policy problems.

H. Improvements of Consultation During Crises

Complaints of lack of consultation have been greatest during international crises, the times when congressional support may be most necessary. Congress might consider the following measures to promote more effective consultation at such times:

1. Designation in advance of a crisis consultation group.—The leadership could appoint a formal or informal group comprised of four to a dozen or more specified leaders, chairmen, and ranking minority Members from each House. The important factor would be making clear in advance the persons in Congress that the President was expected to consult immediately in the event of a crisis.

2. Establishment of a congressional crisis information center.—Such a center could provide more coordinated information to Congress and make it somewhat less dependent on the executive branch for information. It could prepare Members so that time in discussions with executive officials would not be consumed by briefings but could focus on contemplated actions.

3. Tightening the War Powers Resolution.—The War Powers Resolution is the chief legislation dealing with crises that may involve the use of U.S. Armed Forces in hostilities. The consultation provisions have not proved effective but might be strengthened by broadening the circumstances in which consultation is required. They could also be strengthened by specifying the participants.

I. Improvement of Consultation on Multidimensional Problems

Consultation is more difficult on problems that involve international organizations as well as executive branch agencies and that cross several committee jurisdictions in Congress. Coordination of policymaking on such issues in both branches requires further study, but certain options have emerged for promoting more effective consultation:

1. Establish ad hoc consultative committees.—Groups representing all the committees having jurisdiction might be established for consultative, not legislative, purposes. The Members could share differing perspectives on such problems, discuss goals for international negotiations, oversee the negotiations when they occur and form a counterpart to interagency committees from the executive branch.

2. Congressional observers on delegations to international conferences.—Attendance at conferences assists Members in understanding diplomatic problems and provides a timely opportunity for discussions with executive officials conducting the negotiations.

3. Senate confirmation of negotiators.—Senate hearings provide an opportunity for Senators to discuss prospective negotiations in advance with the person nominated to head the American delegation.

4. Informal caucuses.—Informal groups provide a way for interested Members to become informed and discuss subjects with executive officials. If a wide range of Members participate, they may serve a coordinating function on issues that cross committee jurisdiction.

J. CONCLUSION

Foreign policy embarrassments resulting from congressional unwillingness to support some executive branch policies have occurred with increasing frequency since the end of the Vietnam war when Congress began to assert its foreign policy powers. During this same period, the consultation between the two branches has often been ineffective. Building a system of effective consultation offers a promising approach to reducing such foreign policy embarrassments.

Consultation also offers a method to seek a greater consensus on the chief challenges in foreign policy. The executive branch has not made a concerted effort to build public support on major new policies through consultation since the Marshall plan era. There remain many issues on which the need for a more coherent policy with wider national support is widely acknowledged. Such issues include United States-Soviet relations, arms control policy, foreign aid policy, and policy toward Central America. In any of these areas, a major effort by the two branches to agree on future policy through consultation seems warranted.

Effective consultation cannot cure all the problems inherent in the separation of foreign policy powers, particularly on issues where national consensus does not exist. Nevertheless, it does have the potential for capitalizing on the benefits of that system by bringing more perspectives to bear on international problems and strengthening national support.

PART 1. THE MEANING OF CONSULTATION

This part discusses the constitutional separation of powers and the events in recent years that have created interest in improving foreign policy consultation between the two branches. It then explores the various uses of the term and seeks to define effective consultation. Finally, it looks at the potentialities and limitations of consultation with a view to identifying realistic expectations.

I. BACKGROUND

A. CONSTITUTIONAL SHARING OF THE FOREIGN POLICY POWERS

In writing the Constitution, the Founding Fathers divided the foreign policy powers between Congress and the President in such a way that the support of both branches was frequently required for effective foreign policy. Congress was given power to raise and support armies, provide and maintain a navy, and declare war, but the President was made Commander in Chief of the Army and Navy. The President was given the power to receive Ambassadors and other public Ministers, but the appointment of these officials, as well as the making of treaties, was subject to the advice and consent of the Senate. Congress was given the power to lay and collect taxes and duties, pay debts, regulate foreign commerce, and make all necessary and proper laws, while the President was given the Executive power and charged with taking care that the laws be faithfully executed.[1]

While giving the President control of many instruments for carrying out foreign policy, the Founding Fathers intentionally placed congressional checks on his foreign policy powers. Alexander Hamilton wrote in the Federalist papers:

> The history of human conduct does not warrant that exalted opinion of human virtue which would make it wise in a nation to commit interests of so delicate and momentous a kind as those which concern its intercourse with the rest of the world to the sole disposal of a magistrate, created and circumstanced, as would be a president of the United States.[2]

As a result of this separation or sharing of powers, the effective formulation and carrying out of U.S. foreign policy, like domestic policy, depends upon both branches. An obvious example is the making of treaties and laws. The executive branch may negotiate a treaty, but if the Senate does not give its advice and consent, the treaty cannot be ratified. Congress may pass a law establishing a foreign policy measure, but the bill must be signed by the President—or passed over his veto by a two-thirds majority in both Houses—and executed by

---
[1] The powers of the Congress may be found in art. I, sec. 8, of the Constitution. The powers of the President may be found in art. II, secs. 1, 2, and 3.
[2] Hamilton, Alexander. The Federalist No. 75. In Cooke, Jacob E. The Federalist. Middletown, Conn., Wesleyan University Press, 1961, pp. 505–6.

the President in an effective way if the measure is to accomplish its objective.

The necessity of support from both branches for effective foreign policy might seem to make consultation between the two branches an easy thing to achieve. In practice, however, the constitutional division of foreign policy powers has resulted, in the words of Edward S. Corwin, in an "invitation to struggle for the privilege of directing American foreign policy." [3] The relative share of the President and Congress in formulating foreign policy has varied over the years, depending upon the holders of the offices and the issues and circumstances confronting them.

The separation of powers also exists in domestic policy, but the involvement of foreign governments and peoples makes interbranch management of foreign policy more complicated than domestic policy. On issues primarily relating only to the American people, the President and Congress may disagree and hammer out their differences until a solution is reached, and it is "all in the family." On issues that are also being negotiated with foreign countries, executive branch officials are especially concerned that the United States speak with one voice to avoid confusing or misleading foreign peoples, to avoid giving opponents tactical advantage, and to persuade their foreign counterparts that the United States has a coherent and effective foreign policy. No other country has a system in which the legislature is so independent of the executive. Consequently, leaders and publics in other nations have difficulty in understanding the conduct of foreign policy in the United States.

B. Legislative-Executive Confrontations on Foreign policy

In recent years both executive branch officials and Members of Congress have repeatedly complained about the poor coordination of congressional and executive branch activities on important foreign policy decisions and actions. The problem has grown particularly since the early 1970's, when Congress became determined to play its foreign policy role with greater independent vigor. With Congress playing an assertive role, the number of executive-legislative disagreements on foreign policy increased. One writer called the relationship between the President and a more assertive Congress the "weak link, if not the weakest link," in the foreign policymaking process.[4]

During the past decade, there were at least five highly visible legislative-executive confrontations that resulted in serious foreign policy embarrassments for the United States.

(1) The first and most significant confrontation was over when and how to get the United States out of the Vietnam war. This issue mobilized congressional involvement in international issues and is widely considered the beginning of a reassertion of congressional power in foreign policy.[5] After President Nixon on January 23, 1973, announced the signing of the Paris peace accord

---
[3] Corwin, Edward S. The President, Office and Powers, 1787–1957. New York University Press, 1957, p. 171.
[4] Spanier, John, and Joseph Nogee. Congress, the Presidency, and American Foreign Policy. New York. Pergamon Press, 1981, p. x.
[5] A study on the role of Congress in Vietnam is now in process by William Gibbons, Specialist in U.S. Foreign Policy, Congressional Research Service.

ending U.S. involvement in the Vietnam war, attacks by the Khmer Rouge in Cambodia continued and the United States resumed bombing. Against the wishes of the administration, which was attempting to maintain flexibility on what the United States would do if North Vietnam violated the peace accords, Congress passed a measure stating that after August 15, 1973, no funds under any legislation could be used to "finance directly or indirectly combat activities by United States military forces in or over or from off the shores of North Vietnam, South Vietnam, Laos or Cambodia." [6]

(2) In early 1975 Congress imposed an embargo on arms sales to Turkey on the grounds that Turkey, by its military intervention in Cyprus, had violated its agreement with the United States to use American arms for defensive purposes only. The administration strongly opposed the embargo on the grounds it would impair relations with the strategically located NATO ally.[7]

(3) In 1974 the Nixon administration was proceeding with plans to normalize trade with the Soviet Union as part of a move toward détente. Congress adopted amendments to the Trade Act of 1974 limiting the amount of Export-Import Bank credits to the Soviet Union to $300 million and making the granting of most-favored-nation treatment conditional upon its adoption of more liberal emigration policies.[8] On January 14, 1975, the Soviet Union renounced the United States-Soviet trade agreement of 1972, giving among its reasons dissatisfaction with the conditions in the trade agreement.

(4) In early 1976, when the United States was supplying covert assistance through the Central Intelligence Agency to factions in Angola against a movement supported by Cuban troops and Soviet military assistance, Congress prohibited any kind of assistance to Angola unless expressly authorized by Congress, thus forcing the administration to end the aid.[9]

(5) Senate consideration of the SALT II Treaty and Protocol, signed in June 1979, raised so many doubts that action was delayed; in the interim the Soviet Union's invasion of Afghanistan brought about a deferral of consideration for an indefinite period.[10]

In at least three other cases serious embarrassments to U.S. diplomacy were narrowly averted. In one the possibility loomed large that the Senate would refuse to approve treaties that the administration had spent years negotiating and considered key elements of foreign policy. In two others Congress came close to invoking a legislative veto which would have prevented the executive branch from carrying out commitments that it had publicly made to foreign governments.

---

[6] Sec. 108 of the Continuing Appropriations Act, Fiscal Year 1974, approved July 1, 1973. Similar wording was placed in sec. 307 of the Second Supplemental Appropriation Act, Fiscal Year 1973, Public Law 93-50, approved July 1, 1973.
[7] Sec. 620(x) of the Foreign Assistance Act of 1961, as amended by Public Law 93-559, approved Dec. 30, 1974. This case is explored in Congressional-Executive Relations and the Turkish Arms Embargo.
[8] Public Law 93-618, approved Jan. 3, 1975.
[9] 1976 Defense Appropriations Act, Public Law 94-212; the prohibition was also placed in sec. 404, International Security Assistance and Arms Export Control Act of 1976, Public Law 94-329, approved June 30, 1976.
[10] See Congress and Foreign Policy, 1978.

(1) On March 16 and April 18, 1978, after one of the longest debates in history and numerous amendments and reservations, the Senate voted by 68 to 32, only 1 vote more than the required two-thirds, to approve the ratification of the two Panama Canal treaties. The next year, the House of Representatives delayed approval of the implementing legislation until September 26, 1979, only 4 days before October 1 when the treaties were to enter into force and only after rejecting the first conference report.[11]

(2) In 1980 the House passed a resolution of disapproval of President Carter's decision to approve the sale of uranium fuel for India's Tarapur atomic power station. The sale continued because the Senate, voting 46 to 48, failed to support the resolution.[12]

(3) In 1981 the House passed a resolution of disapproval of the sale of an AWACS and F-15 enhancement package to Saudi Arabia. The Senate failed to support the resolution of disapproval by a vote of 48 to 52.[13]

Such confrontations between the executive branch—ultimately the President—and Congress in the foreign policy field clearly threaten damage to U.S. effectiveness abroad. Moreover, when escalated to the center of the national political stage, issues are likely to be resolved more on the relative political power of the President and his congressional opponents than on their merits.

C. Growing Interest in Consultation

Many suggest that the answer is for Congress to recede from its active role. Others believe that the benefits of congressional participation outweigh the disadvantages, and that in any event, Congress has numerous foreign policy functions under the Constitution that it must fulfill. A third group sees confrontation as an inevitable part of the constitutional process. And a fourth group accepts this view and concludes that it is therefore necessary to modify the Constitution so as to assure greater executive branch dominance in foreign policy, or perhaps through establishment of a parliamentary system. Nevertheless, a widely perceived need in the short term to improve the relationship between the two branches in the making of foreign policy has led to growing interest in increasing the effectiveness of consultation between them.

The Murphy Commission, the Commission on the Organization of the Government for the Conduct of Foreign Policy, wrote in its final report in 1975, "a new era of cooperation between the executive and legislative branches in foreign relations is vital to the security of our nation and to the peace of the world." [14] The basic theme of many of its proposals was to seek new ways for the President and Congress to "participate jointly in the formulation and maintenance of policies responsible both to the exigencies of the outer world and the concerns of the American electorate." [15]

---

[11] See Congress and Foreign Policy, 1979.
[12] See Congress and Foreign Policy, 1980.
[13] This case is explored in Executive-Legislative Consultation on U.S. Arms Sales.
[14] Commission on the Organization of the Government for the Conduct of Foreign Policy. Report. June 1975. Washington, U.S. Government Printing Office, 1975, p. 195.
[15] Ibid., p. 197.

The Hamilton subcommittee of the House Foreign Affairs Committee wrote in its report mentioned earlier:

> If the executive branch and Congress are able to agree on what consultation should involve, which Members of Congress are to be consulted, and at what point in the decision-making process consultation ought to occur, the potential for conflict between the two branches can be reduced and a better working relationship can be facilitated.[16]

A wide array of practitioners and scholars have, moreover, looked at the issue with increasing concern.[17] In 1979 two scholars writing a book on the growing role of Congress in foreign policy wrote:

> A better way had to be found, one that permitted early, thorough consultation, a sharing of the decisionmaking process: a system of *policy codetermination*.[18]

This report is a response to the growing interest in consultation. Its next chapter explores the concept of consultation and its potentialities and limitations.

---

[16] Special Subcommittee on Investigations, Congress and Foreign Policy, p. 3.
[17] See Appendix C. Executive-Legislative Relations on Foreign and National Security Policy: A Selected, Annoted Bibliography.
[18] Franck, Thomas M. and Edward Weisband. Foreign Policy by Congress. New York, Oxford University Press, 1979, p. 61.

II. THE IDEAL AND REALITY OF CONSULTATION

There is a great deal of idealization about foreign policy consultation, and a wide gap between the ideal and reality.

When the term is used, many people think nostalgically of President Truman and Secretary of State Acheson inviting Senators Arthur Vandenberg and Tom Connally to discuss the establishment of the United Nations or the Marshall plan or the North Atlantic Treaty. Consultation is viewed as an objective in itself that, if it could be obtained, would produce good foreign policy on which there was national consensus.

The reality is that the executive branch seldom consults effectively with Congress on important foreign policy decisions, and almost never unless it needs to for some specific reason. Today a meeting between the President and one or two Senators usually would not be considered adequate congressional participation. Divisions on some problems are so deep that it is unlikely that they can be resolved by any method except a vote that measures the political strength of each side.

This chapter examines the concept of consultation to find steps between the reality and the ideal.

A. Lack of Adequate Consultation of Congress by the Executive

Consultation might seem to be a two-way problem because it requires each branch to seek the views of the other prior to setting a course that cannot easily be changed. Moreover, both branches can take measures to improve consultation. In important respects, however, the problem is largely one sided. Despite an occasional surprise, ordinarily Congress consults with the executive branch on legislation affecting foreign policy because such consultation is built into the system. One of the first things committees do when considering foreign policy matters is to solicit the views of the Department of State.

The executive branch, on the other hand, for reasons it considers valid, does not ordinarily consult effectively with Congress before making important decisions. This is the essence of the consultation problem.

Repeatedly in the past 20 years the executive branch has taken important foreign policy steps without first seeking the views of Congress. When a legislative-executive confrontation or embarrassment has occurred, close examination reveals that there has not been effective consultation. Often the executive branch took important actions without even discussing them with Members of Congress. Any discussions were usually after the decision was made. A few examples follow.

In the 14 years from 1966 through 1979 when sanctions against Rhodesia were in effect, the executive branch never consulted Congress on the framing of the policy options or the choice among options.[1]

After the 1974 coup on Cyprus which led to the arms embargo on Turkey mentioned earlier as a foreign policy embarrassment, legislative branch members had to "relentlessly pursue the executive for information and to exchange views on emerging policies."[2]

In making the 1978 decision to establish diplomatic relations with the People's Republic of China and end the mutual defense treaty with Taiwan, the administration did not consult Congress despite a provision in legislation making it clear that Congress wanted to be consulted.[3]

In 1981 the chairman of the House Foreign Affairs Subcommittee on Asian and Pacific Affairs complained of finding out from a New York Times reporter about a proposed military aid package for Pakistan. Two hours earlier an administration witness had testified that the administration intended to consult with the subcommittee but did not say that a decision had been made.[4]

In the sale of AWACS and F-15 enhancements to Saudi Arabia in 1981, discussed earlier as nearly resulting in a legislative veto, Congress was not notified until a de facto commitment to Saudi Arabia had been made.[5]

Almost every postwar President has made decisions to use U.S. Armed Forces without consulting Congress in advance but instead informing them after the decision: President Truman in the invasion of South Korea in 1951; President Kennedy in the Cuban missile crisis of 1962; President Johnson in the Dominican Republic in 1965; President Nixon in the bombing of Cambodia of 1969; President Ford in the Mayaguez crisis of 1975; President Carter in the attempt to rescue American hostages from Iran in 1980; and President Reagan in the decision to send Marines to Lebanon in 1982. President Eisenhower came the closest to consulting when, after essentially deciding to send Marines to Lebanon in 1958, he called in congressional leaders to see if there were strong objectives.

Despite calls for improvement, it is difficult to find cases of effective legislative-executive consultation in recent years. The Marshall plan, the North Atlantic Treaty, and the Japanese Peace Treaty from the immediate postwar period remain the best examples of consultation. In those instances, with congressional support clearly necessary, the administration held discussions with appropriate congressional committees and leaders from the outset. In the Marshall plan the administration provided ample time for Congress to study the proposal by establishing an interim aid program to Western Europe. Secretary of State Dean Acheson worked with Senators and Representatives as well as ambassadors of other countries in working out drafts of the North Atlantic Treaty.[6]

---

[1] Copson, Raymond. Sanctions against Rhodesia, p. 10.
[2] Laipson, Ellen. Congressional-Executive Relations and the Turkish Arms Embargo, p. 16.
[3] Sutter, Robert. Executive-Legislative Consultations on China Policy, 1978–79.
[4] Cronin, Richard. Congress and Arms Sales and Security Assistance to Pakistan. In Congress and Foreign Policy, 1981, p. 105.
[5] Grimmett, Richard. Executive-Legislative Consultation on U.S. Arms Sales.
[6] Acheson, Dean. Present at the Creation. New York, Norton and Company, 1969, p. 277.

In the case of the Japanese Peace Treaty the negotiator, John Foster Dulles, met regularly, on an average of more than once a month, with the Senate Foreign Relations consultative subcommittee on the Far East from the day after his confirmation until the treaty was completed. There were also meetings with the full committee on special problems which resulted in the incorporation of committee suggestions into the final text of the treaty.[7]

When more recent instances of effective consultation have been found, they have more often been initiated by Congress than by the executive branch. An example is the Trade Agreements Act of 1979. Some of the credit for the success in securing an international agreement that was readily endorsed by Congress may be attributed to the skill of the negotiator, Robert Straus. On the other hand, the consultation was more of a legislative initiative than an executive one because Congress had built into the Trade Act of 1974 a role for itself, requiring congressional approval of any nontariff codes of conduct agreed to by the U.S. negotiators in the trade negotiations within the framework of the General Agreement of Tariffs and Trade.[8]

B. DEFINITION OF CONSULTATION

Although most people agree on the need for more effective consultation, there is no agreed definition of what consultation means, and people may mean different things when they use the term.

The word "consult" has often been used very loosely to describe virtually any communication with Congress by the executive branch. Some types of communication clearly do not qualify as consultation. Other forms of communication, however, often involve important elements of consultation.

1. Notify, inform, report, or brief.—These suggest the supplying of information but do not imply either an opportunity to discuss or to affect the decision. The executive branch is likely to notify, inform, or report to Congress in writing or by telephone. Briefing is likely to be done in a conference. The supplying of information may lead to consultation if undertaken early enough to affect the decision. Often, however, it is done after a decision. In the Dominican Republic crisis of 1965, for example, President Johnson invited 14 congressional leaders to the White House, informed them of his decision to intervene with Marines, and asked for their support.[9] President Carter wrote in his memoirs that after he had made the decision to launch the Iranian hostage rescue mission, he had his advisers come by "to talk about the question of consulting with Congress."[10]

2. Conduct market research and intelligence.—Sometimes the administration undertakes discussions with Members of Congress aimed at finding out what action they might take or how they might vote. The primary purpose of such discussions is to count votes or deter-

---
[7] U.S. Congress. Senate. Committee on Foreign Relations, Legislative History of Committee on Foreign Relations, 81st Congress. S. Doc. 81–247, p. 30.
[8] Ahearn, Raymond. Congress and Foreign Trade Policy: The Multilateral Trade Negotiations and Trade Reorganization. In Congress and Foreign Policy, 1979.
[9] The Dominican Republic Intervention in 1965: A Case Study of the Congressional Information Problem. Appendix to Executive-Legislative Consultation on Foreign Policy: Strengthening the Legislative Side.
[10] Carter, Jimmy. Keeping Faith, Memoirs of a President. New York. Bantam Books, 1982, p. 71.

mine how to package a proposal. They may be important preludes to consultation if they are undertaken early enough to influence subsequent steps in the policymaking process.

3. Preemptive guess.—On occasion the administration studies the actions of Congress and bases its policy in part on what it believes Congress wants or would accept; this may be among the more potent forms of congressional influence on foreign policy. The device does not provide Members an opportunity to speak for themselves directly on an issue, but it may well have reduced frictions and embarrassments, and the administration may consider that it has consulted Congress because it has taken congressional views into account. An occasion where "second guessing" led to a wrong evaluation occurred in 1977 when President Carter announced his intention to withdraw American ground forces from Korea over a 4- to 5-year period, apparently in the belief that such a withdrawal would be welcomed in Congress. The move met with considerable congressional opposition and the policy was reversed.[11]

4. Persuade, advocate, or lobby.—These words suggest discussions aimed not at obtaining views but at convincing Members of Congress to support an executive branch proposal. Such discussions can contain an element of consultation if there is room for alteration of the policy, but their premise is that the basic decision has already been made. In the case of the AWACS package to Saudi Arabia, members of the Reagan administration and the President himself met with dozens of Members of Congress to discuss the proposal. In the end, however, the equipment package was sold as originally presented.[12]

5. Plan joint strategy and tactics.—These suggest executive branch discussions with the likeminded allies in Congress to discuss methods of getting the administration's position through Congress. Planning strategy and tactics can have important elements of consultation if started early enough to permit congressional allies to be in on the shaping of policy or if the administration position is flexible enough to permit alterations. Consultative aspects are quite selective, however, the discussions being aimed primarily at bringing along other Members of Congress rather than seeking their views. Intermittently throughout the existence of sanctions on Rhodesia, for example, executive branch and legislative supporters of the sanctions held discussions to coordinate efforts to defeat attempts to alter U.S. policy.[13]

6. Bargain and negotiate.—The administration often conducts discussions with Members of Congress toward the end of the legislative process when it realizes that it is not going to get the legislative support it needs without some concessions. The terms suggest an adversarial relationship with the administration seeking to limit damage to its position. Nonetheless, there are clear elements of consultation if the bargaining includes compromises that modify the decision advocated by the administration. The Senate approval of the Panama Canal Treaties in 1978 provide an example of bargaining. The treaties were approved by a vote of 68 to 32, one more than the required two-thirds

---

[11] Collier, Ellen C. Strengthening the Legislative Side. pp. 58–59.
[12] Grimmett, Richard. Arms Sales to Saudi Arabia: AWACS and the F-15 Enhancements. In Congress and Foreign Policy, 1981.
[13] Copson, Raymond W. Sanctions against Rhodesia.

majority, but not until the Carter administration—and Panama—had agreed to a number of important understandings and reservations and two amendments.

7. *Damage limitation.*—When there is danger that a desired measure will not pass Congress, or that Congress will enact an unwanted measure, the executive branch may suddenly begin to discuss alternatives that they would not seriously consider earlier. Such discussions are a form of bargaining or negotiation and may be considered consultation when they involve a search for an acceptable compromise that Congress helps to shape.

EFFECTIVE CONSULTATION

Effective consultation might be defined as involvement of an appropriate representation of Congress in the making of significant foreign policy decisions by the executive branch.

Analysts differ on the types of issues that should involve Congress, the points at which Congress should become actively engaged, and the range of congressional representatives that should be involved. There is little disagreement, however, that to consult effectively involves:
—substantive exchanges with a range of Members representing the relevant congressional decisionmaking bodies;
—exchanges at a time that permits modification of executive branch positions so as in some measure to accommodate congressional concerns;
—exchanges on significant decisions and issues requiring congressional support;
—mutual recognition of the legitimacy of participation of both branches and their problems and responsibilities.

Thus there are four components that make consultation more or less effective according to the quality of each in a particular instance.

The first component is the range of Members consulted. At its best, consultation would involve all relevant subcommittees and committees, the leadership, and individual Members who had particular interest in and influence on the subject at hand. On occasion, it might involve all Members, although this would rarely be feasible or necessary. It clearly is possible, however, for the executive branch to mobilize a a winning coalition—always its goal—through a smaller number of Members. If the executive branch has the skill to identify them, a few representatives of relevant committees and groups, plus Members with power to influence others in an area, may be able to predict the reactions, express the views of their colleagues, and bring about changes in policy in such a way as to constitute effective consultation.

Consultation with any appropriate Members, that is, Members who hold a leadership position or are on relevant committees, even though it is recognized as tokenism, is usually enough to reduce the charge of nonconsultation.

The second component is the timing of the consultation. Ideally, consultation would bring Members of Congress into the process perhaps as early as a problem is identified but not later than the point at which options have been formulated and the decision among them is to be made. But consultation may still be undertaken effectively as long as there is still room for modification of a policy to take into account congressional views.

The third component is the significance of the issues. Ideally, in theory at least some consultation would be undertaken on all foreign policy issues that require the support of Congress through appropriations or any other means. Without being this comprehensive, consultation may still be effective if there is an opportunity for Congress to participate in decisions on the most important questions, especially those involving commitments of large sums of money or the armed forces.

The fourth component is the attitude with which the consultation is undertaken. In its ideal, consultation would be a sincere attempt of the executive branch to discover and consider the views of Congress on the merits of a problem and discuss the options candidly. In practice, consultation can be effective if each side acknowledges the legitimate role of the other and recognizes the problems and responsibilities shaping its actions.

Consultation can generally be improved by strengthening any of these four components. It is better to consult a few Members than none, and it is still more effective to consult Members representing all the relevant committees and interested groups. It is better to inform Members of a decision prior to taking action than not to inform them at all, but it is more effective to discuss the choice of options before the final decision. It is better to consult on any issue than on none, but effective consultation requires discussing the most important issues. Finally, almost any discussions are better than none, but the more they are conducted in a spirit of candor, respect, and understanding, the more effective they will be.

C. POTENTIALITIES AND LIMITATIONS OF CONSULTATION

Another gap between the ideal and reality exists in the potentialities of consultation. Implicit in the request for this study is the premise that consultation can contribute to effective foreign policymaking. However, consultation should not be viewed as a cure-all. It is a tool or technique for developing a foreign policy and support for that policy and like any tool has limitations and potentialities that need to be understood. Moreover, recent empirical evidence is lacking on the effect of consultation on the quality of foreign policy.

DEVELOPING CONGRESSIONAL SUPPORT

Most analysts believe that consultation can increase legislative support for foreign policy on the basis that Members of Congress are more inclined to support policies that they help shape. During the consultative process, administration officials become aware of congressional views and on occasion make modifications.

To illustrate, after effective consultation during the Tokyo round of trade negotiations on nontariff barriers, the Trade Agreements Act of 1979 [14] was approved by the House by a 395-7 vote and in the Sen-

---

[14] Public Law 96-39, approved July 26, 1979. Ahearn, Congress and Foreign Trade Policy, p. 132.

ate by a vote of 90–4. This was despite predictions that so many domestic economic interests were affected that the measure could never pass Congress. As another example, there was effective consultation between the Reagan administration and the House Foreign Affairs and Senate Foreign Relations Committees, on the plan to send U.S. armed forces as part of a Multinational Force and Observers (MFO) to implement the Sinai peacekeeping functions of the Treaty of Peace between Egypt and Israel. The Senate bill to authorize such a force was passed by voice vote on October 7, 1981, and the House bill was approved by a vote of 368 to 13 on November 19, 1981.

Nevertheless, consultation cannot resolve all differences of opinion, assure sound policy, guarantee legislative support for the President, or prevent all confrontations between the President and Congress. Sometimes there are opposite poles of opinion on an issue that cannot be reconciled. In the case of the Panama Canal treaties, for example, consultation could probably not have erased all differences on the fundamental question of whether the United States or Panama should have sovereignty over the Panama Canal. Similarly, fundamental differences of opinion on the SALT II Treaty with the Soviet Union probably could not have been resolved through consultation.

On such issues, the congressional choice between the alternative courses is made through a vote of the entire Congress that is likely to entail a confrontation between the President and congressional opponents. Thus, when a vote on a contentious issue occurs, leadership and politics remain decisive in determining whether the executive branch prevails in the final vote. It was political effort and persuasion, not consultation, that brought a legislative victory for the Presidency in the case of the Panama Canal treaties and implementing legislation and the AWACS and F-14 enhancement package to Saudi Arabia in 1981.

FOCUSING DEBATE ON SUBSTANCE OF THE PROBLEM

A second potentiality of consultation is to focus debate on the merits of the issue rather than respective roles of Congress and the President. To illustrate, Congress focused on the policy issues when debating whether to invoke a legislative veto over President Carter's 1980 decision to send nuclear fuel for India's reactor at Tarapur. The congressional role was not at issue because Members of Congress had been consulting with the administration on nonproliferation for some time and the legislative veto gave Congress a clear vehicle for action.

In the absence of consultation, on several occasions foreign policy debates in Congress have been diverted from the substance of the issue to questions of Presidential versus congressional prerogatives. Following the establishment of diplomatic relations with China, for example, congressional debate often centered on whether the President had the right to terminate the defense treaty with Taiwan without congressional or Senate consent rather than on evaluating the new policy.

On the other hand, there may be issues that executive branch officials would prefer not be debated by Congress at all. On such issues, it might rather have congressional attention diverted by the essentially procedural question of whether Congress should have a role at all.

OBTAINING DIVERSE ADVICE

Consultation does not necessarily mean that the advice is taken. For one thing, often a consulter gets conflicting advice and it would be impossible to follow all courses advocated. On controversial issues virtually every viewpoint may be represented in Congress. Even so, the seeking of opinions may clarify the advantages and disadvantages of various options.

The executive branch uses as an example the consultations it conducted during 1979 concerning arms sales to Morocco. A guerrilla group (the Polisario) challenging Moroccan claims to the former Spanish Sahara increased their activities and began to launch attacks not only in the disputed territory but in Morocco proper. Because Morocco was considered a friend of the United States, the administration was considering ending an informal unwritten ban on arms that could be used in the western Sahara. Before the Department of State had decided its position, officials consulted both the Senate Foreign Relations and House Foreign Affairs Committees on the options in closed hearings. The Senate Foreign Relations Committee by a vote of 6 to 3 recommended that the United States should furnish Morocco with arms suitable for its defense.[15] The chairmen of the Africa Subcommittees in both the House and the Senate committees warned against sending antiguerrilla weapons on the grounds it would alienate a majority of African nations who had indicated support for the Polisario.[16] In this case a compromise position eventually was reached, and both the State Department officials and Members of Congress described the situation as a model of effective consultation. In many cases a compromise cannot be reached and any decision requires going against the advice of some Members.

BUILDING NATIONAL CONSENSUS ON THE BEST COURSE OF ACTION

Consultation cannot guarantee finding the best possible policy, and at times may make policy action more difficult because of any extra time it takes and the larger number of people involved. Congress may insist on more consideration of domestic or even local factors than foreign policy experts believe warranted.

On the other hand, consultation may help find or develop the best possible policy option that has the necessary public support. The fact is that consultation does require time guards against hastily devised policies that have not been thought through. Wider discussion of policy proposals brings in more perspectives and more facts to consider. Although this cannot assure a sound decision on policy, it provides a forum for the testing of ideas.

The executive-legislative dialog helps educate the public on the underlying issues and provides a channel for the views of the various interests that may be affected. Executive branch officials may consider many different points of view on policy proposals, but they do so in private. Congress usually considers subjects openly, encouraging public discussion prior to congressional action.

---

[15] Kendrick, Joseph T. Strengthening executive branch procedures, pp. 49 and 77.
[16] Congress and Foreign Policy, 1979, p. 81.

The classic example is the formation of the Marshall plan. The durability and consistency of the policy toward Europe developed in the postwar period remains an eloquent testimonial to consultation both between the branches and among the nations concerned. The Japanese Peace Treaty similarly formed a strong base for United States-Japanese relations for many years.

IMPROVING RELATIONS BETWEEN BRANCHES

For the most part, consultation is not an end in itself but a means toward building an effective policy. Nevertheless, consultation itself may be an objective to the extent that it represents a satisfactory working relationship between the two branches, constituting a mutual recognition that each branch has a legitimate role to play in foreign policy.

Certainly the cost of lack of adequate consultation has on occasion proved extremely high in terms of impairing relations. Failure of the Nixon administration to consult with Congress during the crisis in Cyprus in 1974 contributed to the decision of Congress to impose the Turkish arms embargo in 1975. Unilateral announcement by the Carter administration at the end of 1978 that it was terminating the mutual defense treaty with Taiwan added to tensions between the branches that led to a court suit. Congress responded to an executive branch decision to vote for U.N. sanctions against Rhodesia by passing a law prohibiting the United States from complete compliance with the sanctions. With little consultation taking place, there were 14 years of legislative-executive tension on the Rhodesia issue.

RISKS ON BOTH SIDES

Finally, consultation may entail some risks for both the executive branch and Congress. For the executive branch, one risk lies in widening the circle of persons having information about problems or proposed actions that it might like to keep confidential. A second risk is that early consultation may provide opponents more time to organize. Early information about, without frank discussions on, the AWACS package to Saudi Arabia may be a case in point. On June 24, 1981, 3 months before the formal notifications of the arms sales were submitted, 54 Senators sent a letter to the President recommending against the sale and a House concurrent resolution in opposition had 222 cosponsors.[17]

Members of Congress risk being put in a position making it difficult to criticize a policy. When taken into the confidence of the administration and given advance or secret information that they cannot reveal, Members may feel additional constraints against speaking out. A second risk for Members of Congress is that they may be held responsible or identified with a policy on which they were consulted, whether or not they actually gave any advice or their advice was taken. When the decision is entirely the product of the executive branch, the President may be held accountable.

---

[17] Grimmett, Richard F. Executive-Legislative Consultation on U.S. Arms Sales, p. 26.

Both branches share the risk that consultation takes time, and if never brought to an end owing to conflicting maneuvers, could lead to an inability to take any action whatever.

In summary, consultation is not risk-free. Indeed, at this point, risks may not be well understood because there has been so little experience with systematic consultation. Further, there are certainly limits on its capacity to improve policy and bring agreement between opposing philosophies. Nevertheless, consultation can provide helpful views and build legislative and public support. It may alleviate some of the problems in foreign policy caused by the separation of powers, allowing each branch to pay its full role in the formulation of foreign policy without losing the benefits of the checks and balance system.

PART 2. PROBLEMS IN THE CONSULTATION PROCESS

The first chapter in this part summarizes six case studies that were undertaken to help understand the process of consultation and the problems involved. The second chapter analyzes the principal impediments to effective consultation that were revealed.

I. SIX CASE STUDIES

The six cases were selected primarily to examine different kinds of consultation experiences:

1. The establishment of diplomatic relations with the People's Republic of China was selected as an example of a high-salience issue and one in which there were vociferous complaints about lack of consultation.

2. The Turkish arms embargo case was chosen because domestic constituencies became a factor and legislative-executive differences created a foreign policy embarrassment for the United States.

3. The Rhodesian sanctions case was selected as one in which it was recognized that Congress had played a clear role but its nature was uncertain.

4. The arms sales case was selected as one in which Congress has attempted through legislation to gain a larger voice in foreign policy decisions.

5. The Dominican Republic intervention illustrates the information problems Congress has in an international crisis.

6. The Marshall plan stands as a model of good consultation.

The first four cases were published in full as separate studies in this series. The latter two were included as appendixes in two functional studies in the series. Reference to additional case studies may be found in the annotated bibliography in appendix C.

A. EXECUTIVE-LEGISLATIVE CONSULTATIONS ON CHINA POLICY, 1978–79 [1]

OUTLINE OF CASE

On December 15, 1978, President Carter made an announcement that on January 1, 1979, the United States would establish diplomatic relations with the People's Republic of China and break its diplomatic ties with the Nationalist Chinese administration on Taiwan. He also

---

[1] Summarized from: U.S. Congress. House. Foreign Affairs Committee. Executive-Legislative Consultations on China Policy, 1978–79. Congress and Foreign Policy Series No. 1. Committee Print by Robert G. Sutter, Specialist in Asian Affairs, Congressional Research Service. Washington, U.S. Government Printing Office, 1980. June 1980, 42 pp.

announced that 1 year later the United States would terminate its defense treaty with Taiwan. Like the public and most officials in the executive branch, Members of Congress were taken by surprise.

Some Members were particularly concerned about lack of consultation on terminating the mutual defense treaty with Taiwan because a few months earlier Congress had passed an amendment expressing the sense of the Congress that the President should consult with Congress before making any policy changes that might affect the mutual defense treaty.[2] A few took steps in reaction which could have had significant consequences. Senator Harry Byrd introduced legislation stating the sense of Congress that approval by the Senate was required for the termination of any mutual defense treaty, but Congress did not take final action on it. Senator Barry Goldwater and other Members of Congress filed suit and on October 17, 1979, District Court Judge Oliver Gasch ruled that President Carter had acted unconstitutionally in taking action to end the security treaty without the approval of either two-thirds of the Senate or both Houses of Congress. The court of appeals overturned Judge Gasch's decision and it was appealed to the Supreme Court. The Supreme Court granted certiorari, vacated the judgment of the court of appeals and ordered the district court to dismiss the complaint. This left the basic question undecided but permitted the Taiwan defense treaty to terminate.

In January 1979 the administration submitted a package of legislation to govern future relations with Taiwan. The bill provided for continuation of unofficial political ties through the establishment of a nonprofit private corporation, the American Institute in Taiwan, with the people on Taiwan still eligible for U.S. military sales. Many in Congress complained that the administration had acted in haste but, after making numerous changes, Congress passed the legislation and in April the Taiwan Relations Act became law.[3] On January 24, 1980, Congress approved the Sino-American trade agreement granting most-favored-nation tariff treatment to China.

BRIEF SUMMARY OF FINDINGS

The administration offered Congress no real consultations on the change in China policy. Members of Congress judged that the President's action was an affront to them, especially since they had written into legislation their desire to be consulted on any action affecting the Taiwan defense treaty.

The action began a renewed period of often contentious congressional-executive relations over China policy. Later in 1979 plans to phase out other accords with Taiwan became known, and many on the congressional side again felt they had been misled by the administration. They were disappointed that there was not more consultation on arms transfers to Taiwan because they felt the legislative history of the Taiwan Relations Act clearly indicated that Congress expected to play a special role.

---

[2] Sec. 26, International Security Assistance Act of 1978. Public Law 95-384, approved Sept. 26, 1978.
[3] Public Law 96-8, approved Apr. 10, 1979.

Congressional suspicions of the administration's information grew. Several congressional sources at the end of 1979 believed that the administration was not telling the truth when it denied any interest in using closer relations with China against the Soviet Union. Even those in favor of the China policy being pursued took special pains to be certain the administration was supplying full information on the issue of providing most-favored-nation tariff treatment for China.

The main reason given by the administration for not consulting with Congress when it established relations with China was that news leaks of the policy might have led to its reversal and possibly have had repercussions on American politics. Executive officials contended that the Chinese leaders preferred secret negotiations, that publicity would have signaled intentions to the Soviet Union, and that the closed doors permitted freer interchange with Taiwan. Some also admitted that the secrecy permitted the administration to avoid "interference" from those in Congress who might use sensitive information for "demagogy" or for personal political reasons. Because of the secrecy, few in the administration were prepared to answer questions about the policy immediately after the announcement or to draft the needed legislation.

Many in Congress accepted the need for a high degree of secrecy but did not feel this precluded seeking the advice of those in Congress with oversight responsibility for Asian affairs. They suspected the administration had something to hide or was using secrecy to hide confusion in its policies.

A second explanation given by administration officials concerned problems in Congress. Some said Congress lacked "responsive leadership" in foreign affairs, had no clear lines of communication, and no set way of enforcement against Members or staff who use sensitive information in unauthorized ways. They indicated the Congress had not defined what was expected in the way of consultation, and that Members needed to be better informed on the issues to take the initiative in getting their views across to the administration. Some complained that congressional officials had a "chip on their shoulder" about China policy, were infringing on executive prerogatives in foreign affairs, and were jeopardizing American interests in China for the sake of personal "pique" or parochial constituent interests.

The case study concluded the consultative process over China policy did not work well in 1978 and 1979 and that serious friction resulted between Congress and the administration. The friction did not lead to a major crisis in United States-Chinese relations, because the majority in Congress were pleased with the substance of United States-China-Taiwan relations which followed. If there were a major failure in United States-China policy, or executive-legislative tensions became worse, China policy or broader U.S. foreign policy could be seriously affected. For the President, author Robert Sutter concluded,

> The clear lesson of the China case is that he must weigh the short-run advantages of forcing through such a policy change without consultations against the risks of exacerbating relations with Congress and fracturing that trust and confidence which he may need for support of programs further down the road.[4]

---
[4] Executive-Legislative Consultations on China Policy 1978–1979, p. 42.

B. CONGRESSIONAL-EXECUTIVE RELATIONS AND THE TURKISH ARMS EMBARGO [5]

OUTLINE OF CASE

On July 20, 1974, Turkey invaded the island of Cyprus after the ruling military junta in Greece supported a coup attempt led by Greek officers against Archbishop Makarios, the head of the government in Cyprus. Many Members of Congress viewed the Turkish intervention as a violation of its agreement with the United States to use American arms for defensive purposes only. The Senate on September 19, 1975, and the House on September 24, passed sense-of-the-Congress statements calling for a termination of military aid to Turkey. In early 1975, after lengthy public debate, Congress legislated an embargo on arms sales to Turkey which went into effect on February 5, 1975.[6] The administration opposed the embargo on the grounds that it would impair relations with Turkey, an important and strategically located ally in the North Atlantic Treaty Organization.

On May 19, 1975, the Senate voted to lift the embargo if the President felt it would improve the prospects of a solution. The House Foreign Affairs Committee voted to permit commercial trade and to ship goods contracted for prior to the embargo, but the bill was defeated on the House floor. Subsequently, on July 26, the Turkish Government closed U.S. bases and intelligence-gathering facilities in Turkey.

Within days the Senate again passed a bill to lift the embargo, but the chairman of the Rules Committee in the House was opposed and the bill did not reach the floor before the August recess. After the August recess, the House reversed itself and voted in favor of a partial lifting of the embargo which permitted Turkey to make commercial purchases and to be eligible for credits and loans for military sales.[7] The measure also called for the President to report to Congress every 60 days on progress on a Cyprus settlement.

Three years later, on April 2, 1978, the Carter administration sought a lifting of the arms embargo without a direct link to progress by Turkey in finding a solution to the Cyprus situation. On May 3 the House Foreign Affairs Committee voted to lift the embargo and on August 1 the full House agreed, adopting language requiring the President to certify that Turkey was acting in good faith to achieve a settlement. In May the Senate Foreign Relations Committee rejected the proposal, but after hearings by the Armed Services Committee on the defense aspects, the Senate on July 26, 1978, also voted to repeal the embargo.[8] The President made the required certification, and the embargo was lifted.

BRIEF SUMMARY OF FINDINGS

The heated controversy over the Turkish embargo reflected strong differences of opinion, both between the executive and legislative

---

[5] Summarized from: U.S. Congress. House. Foreign Affairs Committee. Congressional Executive Relations and the Turkish Arms Embargo. Committee Print, Congress and Foreign Policy Series No. 3. By Ellen B. Laipson, Analyst in Middle East and North African Affairs, Congressional Research Service. Washington, U.S. Government Printing Office, 1981. June 1981. 60 pp.
[6] Sec. 620(x) of the Foreign Assistance Act, as amended. Public Law 93-559, approved Dec. 30, 1974.
[7] Public Law 94-104, approved Oct. 6, 1975.
[8] Public Law 95-384, approved Sept. 26, 1978.

branches, and within each branch that had existed for several years over U.S. policy toward Greece, Turkey, and Cyprus. The public discord contributed to developments that were destabilizing for the region and undesirable for U.S. policy.

The context surrounding the events was crucial. The time when the embargo was imposed was one of unusual tension between branches stemming both from the Watergate investigation and the assertion of congressional power in foreign policy that accompanied the end of the war in Vietnam.

Some of the conflicts over policy were exacerbated by personalities, especially that of Henry Kissinger. Kissinger tried to manage the related crisis in an individual and private manner. Many Members of Congress felt thwarted in their attempts to consult on the situation. A Secretary of State more inclined to bring Congress into the decisionmaking process might not have drawn such opposition.

The leadership in both branches was an important factor. During the Turkish arms embargo there were leadership crises in both the executive branch and Congress. The Presidency was under severe challenge as a result of Watergate. In the State Department, policy decisions were made by the Secretary with little reference to working level analyses of the international and congressional situations. In Congress, party leaders and committee chairmen were startled at the passion and persuasive powers of a few.

Timing proved important. If congressional concerns had been handled quickly and effectively by the State Department, negative attitudes in Congress might not have developed, and some Members might have voted differently.

The executive and legislative branches had different perceptions of the domestic interest in the policy. Some Members of Congress associated the alleged Turkish violation of their agreement to use U.S. supplied weapons only for defense with perceived violations of law in the Watergate scandal and felt a strict enforcement imperative. Many in the administration believed that a group of politically active Greek-Americans were distorting the congressional view. Executive branch contempt of parochialism in Congress was matched by congressional presumptions of executive officials' disregard for the law.

The importance of the ethnic interest group in the situation was probably exaggerated by outside observers and the executive branch may have enhanced the group's effectiveness by emphasizing its role. While the efforts of some Greek-American organizations was prodigious, the legislation passed reflected multiple congressional motives. In addition, the interaction of Congress and the ethnic groups went both ways, with Members of Congress not only working to achieve the goals of the lobby but also using the lobby as an outside network of political support for action in aid of purposes that went beyond the interests of the Greek-American community.

Institutional factors in both branches had an impact. In the State Department, the country desks for Turkey, Greece, and Cyprus were reassigned in the spring of 1974 from the Near East Bureau to the Europe Bureau, causing dislocations in relationships and the assignment of persons unlikely to be familiar with the earlier problems in

Cyprus. In Congress, many in the House appeared to be concerned primarily with Turkey's transgressions while many in the Senate were more concerned with Secretary Kissinger's perceived failings.

The Turkish arms embargo, partially lifted in 1975 and removed in 1978, failed to achieve one of its main objectives of removing Turkish troops from the island. There is still no consensus on where to place the responsibility. The embargo was a congressional initiative that administration officials and congressional opponents continue to see as contrary to national interests and a misuse of congressional power in foreign policy. Congressional embargo supporters hold the administration partially responsible on grounds of improper implementation of the embargo and because it did not use the congressional embargo threat in its negotiations with Turkey.

The case illustrated that it is difficult for Congress to send subtle signals that are a vital part of international diplomacy, but it also illustrated the real power that Congress can exert. The author, Ellen Laipson, concluded,

The Turkish arms embargo illustrates the persisting difference in defining national interests and U.S. policy by some in Congress and the more centrally controlled executive branch. To make those differences a constructive and positive part of the democratic process in this case required strong leadership from the executive and a willingness to consult early and thoroughly with a Congress that can contribute its sensitivity to public opinion and its natural skills in compromise and accommodation to the forging of American foreign policy.[9]

C. CONSULTATIONS BETWEEN CONGRESS AND THE EXECUTIVE BRANCH ON THE SANCTIONS AGAINST RHODESIA [10]

OUTLINE OF CASE

The United Kingdom refused to grant independence to Rhodesia when other African nations were becoming free because its white minority government did not allow full participation by the black majority. On November 11, 1965, the Rhodesian Government under Prime Minister Ian Smith issued its Unilateral Declaration of Independence. The United Kingdom took the issue to the United Nations Security Council, and in December 1966, the U.N. Security Council found the situation a threat to peace and imposed economic sanctions against Rhodesia.[11] The sanctions included prohibitions against the importation of a wide range of goods from Rhodesia and the sale of arms, ammunition, and petroleum to Rhodesia. In May 1968 the sanctions were extended to prohibit all trade except the export of medical supplies and educational materials to Rhodesia, and to prohibit the entry of holders of Rhodesian passports except for humanitarian purposes. These resolutions imposing sanctions were implemented in the United States through Executive orders issued by President Johnson,

---

[9] Congressional-Executive Relations and the Turkish Arms Embargo, p. 35.
[10] Summarized from: U.S. Congress. House. Committee on Foreign Affairs. Executive-Legislative Consultation on Foreign Policy: Sanctions Against Rhodesia. Committee Print. Congress and Foreign Policy Series No. 6. By Raymond W. Copson, Specialist in International Relations, Congressional Research Service. Washington, U.S. Government Printing Office, September 1982. 69 pp.
[11] Security Council resolutions establishing sanctions under chapter VII of the United Nations Charter are considered binding on members. The United States is protected by the right of veto against resolutions which it opposes becoming binding, but in the Rhodesian case voted in favor.

acting under the authorization in the United Nations Participation Act.

One of the items banned from import under the sanctions was chromium, a metal essential in the making of hardened steels with important military and industrial applications. The principal alternative supplier of chrome at the time was the Soviet Union. In 1971 Congress passed an amendment that prohibited the President, as of January 1, 1972, from banning the importation of any strategic material from any non-Communist country so long as the importation of such materials from Communist countries was not also prohibited. Although Rhodesia was not mentioned, supporters made clear that the purpose of the amendment, known as the "Byrd amendment" after its sponsor, Senator Harry F. Byrd, was to allow the importation of chromium from Rhodesia. Several congressionally sponsored attempts during the Nixon and Ford administrations to repeal the Byrd amendment failed. On March 18, 1977, during the Carter administration, the amendment was modified so that it did not apply to Rhodesia.

The next year, on March 3, 1978, Ian Smith and three black political leaders in Rhodesia signed an agreement in Salisbury, called the "internal settlement," under which the parties agreed to a new constitution and elections to bring in a black Prime Minister while allowing whites to retain considerable economic and political power. Certain black nationalist factions that had launched a guerrilla war in Rhodesia rejected the settlement. Opinion in Congress remained divided. Some favored ending the sanctions, arguing that the Rhodesian authorities had made all the concessions that could reasonably be expected, but others felt that the fact that this internal settlement would essentially permit the continuation of minority white rule precluded normal trade relations. The administration policy was to maintain U.S. adherence to the sanctions until there was an internationally recognized negotiated settlement.

In August 1978, Congress passed an amendment requiring the President to lift the sanctions by December 31 if two conditions had been met by that time: First, the Rhodesian Government had demonstrated its willingness to negotiate at an all-parties conference held under international auspices; and second, that a government chosen by free elections in which all groups had been allowed to participate freely (with verification by impartial, internationally recognized observers) had been installed.

On March 1, 1979, Senators McGovern and Hayakawa jointly introduced a concurrent resolution to send a team of congressionally sponsored, nongovernmental observers to the Rhodesian elections. The resolution passed the Senate, but a similar measure was rejected in the House Africa Subcommittee. The April 22 elections in Rhodesia, in which the party of Bishop Abel Muzorewa won 67 percent of the vote, brought more calls in Congress for the ending of sanctions. In subsequent months, the Senate voted to repeal the sanctions, but the House passed a bill leaving the final decision on lifting the sanctions to the President.

Before final action on the measures took place in Congress, international events resolved the controversy. The new British Government of Prime Minister Margaret Thatcher convened a conference of all the

Rhodesian parties at Lancaster House in London on September 10, 1979, and the Lancaster House talks led to a settlement and the lifting of sanctions by the end of 1979.

BRIEF SUMMARY OF FINDINGS

The sanctions against Rhodesia were a source of legislative-executive tension for more than 14 years, through four administrations and eight Congresses. Except for a brief period during the first months of the Carter administration, the issue was marked by disagreement and mutual lack of confidence. There were strong congressional feelings on both sides of the issue, but both opponents and proponents of the sanctions were dissatisfied with executive branch relations.

At first congressional interest was limited and the executive branch saw no need for consultation. Later, as congressional opposition mounted, the executive branch saw consultations were necessary because Congress was a potential source of trouble for the policy it wanted to carry out. In the final years of the controversy, congressional opposition to the sanctions had grown strong enough that the consultations became a bargaining process which produced minor concessions while permitting the basic policy to be preserved. When the Carter administration in mid-1979 undertook a full-scale campaign to prevent legislation that would have ended the sanctions, it was able to achieve compromises satisfactory to many congressional critics.

Those in Congress and the executive branch who took an active role on the issue held negative images of each other, and their attitudes hampered the establishment of an effective congressional-executive working relationship. Executive branch officials often felt congressional involvement was hasty, based on inadequate information conducive of poor policy in the United Nations and Africa, and outside the prerogative of Congress. Members of Congress who were critics of the sanctions often felt the issue demonstrated not only poor policy judgment by the executive branch but its determination to refuse a legitimate congressional role. Supporters of the sanctions felt the issue provided an example of the unwillingness or the inability of the executive branch to use consultation to gain support of an important foreign policy.

From the beginning Congress was never consulted by the executive branch on the framing of the policy options or the choice among options. The executive branch did engage in two kinds of discussions with Congress: One, campaigns of persuasion that included strategy sessions with allies in Congress; and two, bargaining sessions with opponents aimed at minimizing concessions. Such sessions came only in relation to developments in Congress or Rhodesia. The executive branch never undertook a long-term program to develop congressional support. Instead it adopted a damage-control approach. The executive branch position prevailed over the years with this minimal consultation approach but at the cost of much acrimony.

Several different factors hampered executive branch efforts. There were many other situations throughout the world that seemed more critical, including wars in Vietnam and the Middle East and changing relations with the Soviet Union and China, so that the Rhodesian problem was usually given a low priority until the Carter administration. Limitations on resources restricted the State Department's ability to work with Congress. In addition, efforts of the State Department during the Nixon administration were undermined by a perception in Congress that the White House did not fully support the sanctions.

The author, Ray Copson, states:

> The experience of the Rhodesian sanctions debate suggests that Congress is not likely to be fully satisfied that there has been adequate consultation unless it is brought in on the framing of policy options and on the choice among options. The policymaking prerogative, however, will be closely guarded by the executive branch. In the Rhodesian case, concessions to congressional attempts to play a role in policymaking were made reluctantly, and usually only when the executive saw minor concessions as necessary in order to preserve an overall line of policy. If Congress had been given a major role in the making of Rhodesia policy, however, not every Member of Congress would have been satisfied with the outcome. Objections would no doubt still have been heard from those who felt that the policy choices made after consultations were incorrect.[12]

D. EXECUTIVE-LEGISLATIVE CONSULTATIONS ON U.S. ARMS SALES [13]

OUTLINE OF CASE

In an effort to encourage consultation and increase its participation, Congress passed legislation in 1974 permitting it to veto, by concurrent resolution, major sales of defense articles and services. This legislation was stimulated by a widespread feeling in Congress that despite numerous reporting requirements that had been passed in the 1960's, Congress usually learned of arms sales or transfer proposals too late to affect the decisions.

In the 8 years since the legislative veto was passed, there have been five particularly serious controversies regarding prospective arms sales. In the first three cases a resolution of disapproval never came to a vote on the floor of either House of Congress, and Congress was able to use the threat of a potential veto to promote consultations and bring about compromises or better justifications on the part of the executive branch. In 1978, the Senate rejected a resolution of disapproval on an arms sales package, but the House did not vote on it because the Senate action precluded passage of a concurrent resolution. In 1981, the House voted to disapprove the sale of AWACS and associated F-15 equipment to Saudi Arabia but the Senate narrowly rejected it. Thus, Congress moved closer to effecting a legislative veto but never imposed one.

Following is a brief synopsis of the five cases:

(1) In 1975 the Ford administration notified Congress of a proposed sale to Jordan of the Hawk and Vulcan air defense systems. The House Foreign Affairs Committee reported a resolution of disapproval and the administration temporarily withdrew the proposal. After conferring with opponents of the sale,

---
[12] Sanctions against Rhodesia, p. 3.
[13] Summarized from: U.S. Congress. House. Foreign Affairs Committee. Executive-Legislative Consultations on U.S. Arms Sales. Congress and Foreign Policy Series No. 7. Committee print by Richard F. Grimmett, Specialist in National Defense, Congressional Research Service. December 1982. Washington, U.S. Government Printing Office, 1982. 39 pp.

the administration agreed to place restrictions on the missile system; namely, that they would be permanently installed at fixed sites as defensive and nonmobile antiaircraft weapons.

(2) In 1976 the Ford administration notified Congress of a proposed sale to Saudi Arabia of 1,000 Sidewinder missiles and 1,500 Maverick air-to-surface missiles. Negotiations between branches led to a reduction in the number of Sidewinder missiles from 1,000 to 850 and the Maverick missiles from 1,500 to 650. Even so, the Senate Foreign Relations Committee adopted a resolution of disapproval. Senator John Sparkman, chairman of the committee, obtained a unanimous-consent resolution to return the resolution to the committee, and the resolution was not again reported out, so the sale proceeded.

(3) In 1977 the Carter administration notified Congress that it proposed to sell seven airborne warning and control system (AWACS) aircraft to Iran. Considerable opposition to the sale developed in both the House and Senate, and the House Foreign Affairs Committee approved a resolution of disapproval. The President withdrew the proposal but resubmitted it, with administration witnesses stating that assurances that had been requested by the Senate Foreign Relations Subcommittee on Foreign Assistance had been agreed to by Iran. Neither the House nor Senate took further action to stop the sale.

(4) In 1978 the Carter administration notified Congress of a proposal to sell 60 F-15 fighters to Saudi Arabia in a package with two other sales: 15 F-15 and 75 F-16 aircraft to Israel and 50 F5E aircraft to Egypt. There was a strong suggestion that if Congress blocked one portion of the sale, the administration would withdraw the other. A resolution of disapproval was defeated on a tie vote in the Senate Foreign Relations Committee which then voted to send a new resolution of disapproval to the floor without a committee recommendation. After extensive debate and a secret session, the Senate rejected the resolution of disapproval by a vote of 44-54, so the sale was cleared. Prior to the Foreign Relations Committee action, however, Secretary of Defense Harold Brown sent a letter assuring the Senate that the administration did not intend to sell any other systems or armaments that would increase the range or enhance the offensive capability of the F-15.

(5) In 1981 the Reagan administration notified Congress that it was selling to Saudi Arabia both AWACS and items that would enhance the capabilities of the F-15's that had been sold in 1978, including tanker aircraft, conformal fuel tanks, and missiles. The House voted to disapprove the sales by a vote of 301 to 11, marking the first time either House had voted to disapprove an arms sale since the legislative veto provision had been added. Although 50 Senators had at one time indicated they would cosponsor a resolution of disapproval, the Senate narrowly rejected it after the President's vigorous personal intervention and his signing a letter of certification relating to some of the concerns of Senators. The sale was thus cleared although there had not been any substantial change in the content of the package.

BRIEF SUMMARY OF FINDINGS

Since the early 1970's, arms sales have become a major element of U.S. foreign policy and therefore Congress has attempted to increase its role in the process of making decisions on arms sales. The executive branch has resisted this effort, considering it an intrusion into the executive branch's carrying out of foreign policy.

Despite congressional use of reporting requirements and the legislative veto, the executive branch has "almost always found ways of finessing detailed consultations with Congress on major arms sales until it has made its basic decision to sell." [14]

Congress added the legislative veto provision to arms sales legislation in 1974 with the intention of providing Congress with power to block a sale and thus to assure that the administration would consult with Congress before committing itself to a sale. Later it added requirements for an annual preview of expected arms sales and negotiated an additional 20-day informal notification in an attempt to encourage the executive branch to consult with Congress before it made any commitment to a foreign country for a sale. The congressional hope was that earlier consultations would permit Congress to disapprove or call for modification of a sale before such action would cause an embarrassment to the executive branch.

While at first Congress was able to use the threat of a legislative veto to force consultation in a manner that led to changes in the numbers or types of items proposed for sale, in more recent years, it has not been able to do this as successfully. When a veto resolution has actually come to a vote, the President has demonstrated the ability to define the issue in a way that makes it extremely difficult to overrule his decision. He has been able to defeat serious criticisms of the merits of the sales proposals by arguing that the national security, or bilateral relations with an important nation, or the basic power of the Presidency would be damaged.[15]

The author, Richard F. Grimmett, concludes,

> In spite of the inherent capability of the President to dominate the critical phases of the debate over an arms sale case, it is likely that most executive branch consultations with Congress on controversial sales will be conducted with the intent of minimizing potential divisiveness on a given sale. Most Presidents are not likely to seek a confrontation with Congress to achieve a policy objective that can be obtained by carefully timed and "creative" consultations. But should such a confrontation occur, it appears at this time that the President has regained the upper hand in the continuing struggle over the process of making arms sales. It appears that only further tightening of existing reporting requirements or the actual exercise of a legislative veto by the Congress might restore the power balance in this policy area, and, perhaps, lead to the kinds of early consultative involvement in the decisionmaking process that congressional critics of the existing procedures seek.[16]

---

[14] Ibid., p. 3.
[15] Note by Richard F. Grimmett, June 30, 1983: Subsequent to the publication of this case study, the Supreme Court, on June 23, 1983, held that a one-House legislative veto in the Immigration and Naturalization Act was unconstitutional. The reasoning supporting the Court's conclusion appears to have adverse implications for the arms sales veto by concurrent resolution. At this time it is unclear what the long-term effect of the loss of the legislative veto will have on executive-legislative consultation in the arms sales area (assuming that the President's authority to sell arms survives an adverse ruling on the veto). It may be that the President's effective authority to make arms sales he wishes will be significantly strengthened now that the threat of a veto by a simple majority of the Congress has been removed. On the other hand, if the President pursues an overly assertive approach to Congress in this policy area, he could stimulate an institutional reaction that could result in enactment of legislation more tightly restricting his legal authority to make arms sales.
[16] Executive-Legislative Consultations on U.S. Arms Sales, p. 39.

E. THE DOMINICAN REPUBLIC INTERVENTION IN 1965: A CASE STUDY OF THE CONGRESSIONAL INFORMATION PROBLEM [17]

OUTLINE OF CASE

After the overthrow in 1961 of the Trujillo regime which had been in control of the Dominican Republic for more than 30 years, national elections were held in 1962 and Juan Bosch became President. Bosch was overturned in a military coup, and the United States recognized the postcoup regime in December 1963. Donald J. Reid Cabral became the new President, and elections were scheduled for September 1965. Former Presidents Juan Bosch and Joachim Balaguer both announced from exile their intentions to run in the elections.

On April 22, 1965, Reid discovered a military plot and dismissed the officer involved. This served as a catalyst for a coup beginning April 24. On April 26 the anti-Bosch military faction asked for U.S. troops to defeat the rebellion. On April 27, President Johnson announced the evacuation of Americans and on April 28, after a second request for assistance, 500 American marines landed in Santo Domingo.

Within about 10 days there were 23,000 American troops in the Dominican Republic. On May 5 a cease-fire was arranged by a commission sent to Santo Domingo by the Organization of American States. An Inter-American Peace Force was created to restore peace, with the United States providing the majority of troops but other countries also participating. U.S. forces remained nearly 17 months.

Throughout that period there was considerable debate in Congress about the need and reasons for the intervention. The majority of the House demonstrated support for the administration's policy by approving by a vote of 312 to 52 a resolution stating the sense of the House that in case of subversion or threat of subversion, any of the parties to the Inter-American Treaty of Reciprocal Assistance could resort to armed force to forestall or combat international communism in the Western Hemisphere.[18] Some in Congress, on the other hand, strongly criticized the administration, both for the substance of the policy pursued and for the nature of the information provided Congress.

BRIEF SUMMARY OF FINDINGS

The situation in the Dominican Republic illustrates the problems for Congress in obtaining and interpreting information and making a contribution to policy decisions during a fast-moving international crisis.

There was discussion between the President and Congress during the crisis, some at the initiative of the executive branch. On April 28, President Johnson telephoned Senator Richard Russell, chairman of the Senate Armed Services Committee, about the situation and in the evening called a meeting of 14 Members of Congress. He informed them of his decision and asked for their support which they gave. Although accounts of the meeting later differed, the initial reason given for the intervention seemed to emphasize the need to protect American lives.

---

[17] Summarized from The Dominican Republic Intervention in 1965: A Case Study of the Congressional Information Problem. By Martha Crenshaw Hutchinson. In U.S. Congress. House. Committee on Foreign Affairs. Executive-Legislative Consultation on Foreign Policy: Strengthening Foreign Policy Information Sources for Congress. Congress and Foreign Policy Series No. 4. Committee Print, February 1982. Washington, U.S. Government Printing Office, 1982, pp. 73–84.
[18] House Resolution 560, adopted Sept. 20, 1965.

On May 2 the President met again with congressional leaders and briefed them on the situation, just before a public speech, now emphasizing the purpose of preventing a Communist regime in the Dominican Republic. On May 4 the President met with the House and Senate Committees on Armed Services, Appropriations, and Foreign Affairs and Foreign Relations to request additional military appropriations for Vietnam and the Dominican Republic, saying that if the request were not approved, the Government would use a temporary transfer authority from another account.

Legislative-executive discussions were also held at the initiative of the Congress. In July the Senate Foreign Relations Committee held hearings that were a direct and formal request for information and analysis. Interpretations of the information provided varied widely and apparently, in some cases, according to preconceived political viewpoints. Holding the hearings in executive session complicated the information problem for the public and Congress, and some Senators complained that committee procedures for using the information hampered access to it. In addition, the public was unable to judge the competing interpretations.

On the major issues of whether the intervention was necessary to prevent Communist expansion, opinion in Congress was sharply divided. In debating the issue, Members expressed suspicion and distrust of accuracy of information provided by the executive branch and from outside. Some Members felt the executive branch had exhibited a lack of candor in communicating its view of the situation, whereas others accepted the administration's case and accused critics of bias and distortion of the facts.

The author, Martha Crenshaw Hutchinson, concluded:

> The Dominican case indicates that one of the main problems in obtaining information either about executive branch intentions or about objective situations is the impartiality and reliability of the information sources. When Congress agrees with administration policy aims, it tends to regard information from the executive branch as trustworthy. However, when there is policy disagreement, charges of lack of candor and cooperation increase. A more independent civil service might help solve this problem. In any case, any independent source of information to be used by Congress must be both highly-respected and politically neutral. Interpretations of information may differ, but if the information relied upon is accurate, then differences of opinion are legitimate rather than misinformed.[19]

F. THE MARSHALL PLAN MODEL [20]

OUTLINE OF CASE

On June 5, 1947, Secretary of State George Marshall gave an address calling for U.S. assistance to help Europe rebuild its wartorn economy if the Europeans initiated and agreed on a plan for recovery. The Western European countries immediately responded. They established a Committee of European Economic Cooperation and developed a 4-year program for European economic recovery.

---

[19] The Dominican Republic Intervention in 1965, p. 84.
[20] Summarized from: The Marshall Plan Model: A Case Study of the Congressional Information Problem by Martha Crenshaw Hutchinson. Appendix in: U.S. Congress. House. Committee on Foreign Affairs. Executive-Legislative Consultation on Foreign Policy: Strengthening the Legislative Side. Congress and Foreign Policy Series No. 5. Committee Print, April 1982. Washington, U.S. Government Printing Office, 1982, pp. 77–85.

Meanwhile, conditions worsened in Europe and in the fall of 1947, President Truman asked Congress to approve an emergency interim aid program. In December Congress passed the Foreign Aid Act of 1947 authorizing the interim assistance.

On December 19, 1947, President Truman sent the proposal for the European recovery program to Congress. Prior to presentation of the program the administration had appointed three special committees to study different aspects of the program. One of the committees, the President's Committee on Foreign Aid, directed by Secretary of Commerce Averell Harriman and comprised of distinguished private citizens of both parties, had been formed in part at the suggestion of Senator Arthur Vandenberg at a consultation at the White House after the Marshall plan speech. All three committees issued their report before Congress held hearings on either the interim aid or the long-term aid proposal. Although the reports differed in some ways, they indicated a consensus that to avoid economic collapse the Western European countries needed assistance; that with assistance Europe could recover, and that if assistance were not given, free institutions could be in jeopardy.

The executive branch prepared a great deal of material for congressional consideration of the subject, and the information supplied was widely praised in Congress.

So that all the factfinding would not be confined to the executive branch, the House created a Select Committee on Foreign Aid to go abroad and make an independent study. House Foreign Affairs Committee Chairman Charles A. Eaton was also chairman of the select committee. Vice-Chairman Christian A. Herter headed the overseas mission. Members visited every nation in Europe except the Soviet Union, Yugoslavia, and Albania, and interviewed both private citizens and Government officials. Many of the committee's recommendations were incorporated in the final version of the Marshall plan. Other congressional groups also made studies.

Both Houses held relatively brief hearings on the interim aid program but lengthy and comprehensive hearings on the European recovery program. Relations between the Truman administration, particularly the Department of State, and the Foreign Relations Committee were excellent. In the spring of 1948 the program was readily approved by Congress, the Senate voting 69 to 17 and the House 329 to 74 in favor of the act.

BRIEF SUMMARY OF FINDINGS

The enactment of the legislation establishing the Marshall plan was one of the best examples of bipartisan cooperation in the postwar period. Although the executive branch was under the control of the Democrats and Congress was under the control of the Republicans, an innovative foreign policy program involving large appropriations was launched. The amount and quality of the information supplied to Congress for its consideration of the program was unprecedented.

Four factors were particularly important to the successful cooperation.

> (1) The postwar situation was unique and compelling; agreement that action was urgently needed to prevent the economic collapse of Europe and a Communist takeover was widespread.

(2) There was close collaboration between Senator Arthur Vandenberg, a Republican leader and chairman of the Senate Foreign Relations Committee, and the Democratic administration.

(3) Congress had ample time to judge the plan. Since funds were needed, the executive branch was eager to encourage congressional approval. When it decided that some emergency aid was needed immediately, the administration did not rush approval of the longer range program but instead devised an interim program, for which it also asked congressional approval.

(4) Congress conducted a lengthy study of the program and developed independent sources of information.

The author, Martha Crenshaw Hutchinson, concluded that it was unlikely that the circumstances would often reoccur and that the Marshall plan constituted an ideal more than a norm of legislative-executive cooperation in the making of foreign policy. The factors suggested that Congress would find it useful to look outside the executive branch for objective evaluations of events and alternatives to policy. In addition, she said:

> Executive willingness to provide comprehensive information and the expanse of time Congress was given to consider legislation, were partially results of executive dependence on Congress for authorization of funds and of uncertainty as to the outcome of the legislation. If the executive branch is sure of a majority of congressional support or can act without congressional knowledge or support, information is likely to be less readily supplied.[21]

---

[21] Ibid., p. 85.

II. IMPEDIMENTS TO CONSULTATION

Why does the executive branch fail to consult effectively with Congress on foreign policy? This study found seven parallel problems in the executive and legislative branches that serve as impediments.

A. ATTITUDES ON ROLE OF CONGRESS IN FOREIGN POLICY

Within the executive branch, the greatest barrier to consultation appears to be the attitude that congressional participation in foreign policy should be kept to a minimum. Even when it is clear that carrying out a policy requires congressional action, such as Senate advice and consent to a treaty or the authorization and appropriation of funds, administrations normally frame their policy proposals before serious discussions with Congress begin, and then lobby for acceptance of those proposals with little or no change.

Foreign policymakers in the executive branch are generally unsympathetic to arguments that either the constitutional role of Congress or the practical value of taking early soundings on congressional opinion provide persuasive reasons to consult early and widely. State Department officials typically believe that foreign policy should be made by the professionals, the career experts, and note that minimal consultation has worked quite well over time. Their experience has left them skeptical of the value of political views or the substantive contribution that some Members may be able to make.

A classic case of the executive branch approach in this regard was the Convention on the Law of Treaties, signed for the United States on April 24, 1970. Despite the obvious institutional interest of the Senate in international law on treaties, there appears to have been almost no legislative consultation prior to signature. The treaty remains pending in the Senate Foreign Relations Committee because the committee and the Department of State were unable to agree on an understanding proposed by the committee to deal with executive agreements.[1]

There are also attitudinal barriers on the legislative side. Members of Congress are frequently uncertain of their role and cautious in their judgments on foreign policy matters, even when the top policymakers in the executive branch have little or no more experience in foreign policy than they do. Though decisions of the President on a foreign policy issue may be challenged by some in Congress, many refrain from open opposition to the President out of a reluctance to cause the Nation embarrassment, even if they question the wisdom of the decision. In two cases when the House had passed resolutions of disapproval— the shipment of nuclear fuel to India in 1980 and the AWACS sale to Saudi Arabia in 1981—Presidents Carter and Reagan, respectively, successfully appealed to this reluctance among Members of the Senate.

---

[1] Executive L 92-1, pending on the Senate Foreign Relations Committee calendar. For text of proposed understanding, see Rovine, Digest of United States Practice in International Law, 1974, p. 195.

Other Members believe they should avoid participation in foreign policy formulation because of the fear of being coopted by the executive branch and losing their independence of perspective and their critical posture.

The Hamilton committee report warned,

* * * no matter how routinized and accepted a practice consultation might become, Members of Congress need to be wary of the tendency to be co-opted by the executive branch. Consultation should not preempt the congressional role as critic and overseer of the executive branch. A degree of balance between the confrontation generated by an historical adversary relationship and the co-optation risked by close relations with the executive branch must always be the goal.[2]

A few view the whole period from the end of World War II through the early part of the Vietnam war as a period in which Presidents used consultation as a tool for coopting Congress to support their foreign policies such as the Marshall plan, the establishment of the United Nations, and the Japanese Peace Treaty.

The classic case cited by such critics is the passage of the Gulf of Tonkin Resolution following two attacks by North Vietnam on U.S. ships in the Gulf of Tonkin,[3] President Johnson called in congressional leaders and told them "that I believed a congressional resolution of support for our entire position in Southeast Asia was necessary and would strengthen our hand."[4] After the formal request for such a resolution on August 5, 1964, Congress passed it within 2 days affirming that the United States was "prepared, as the President determines, to take all necessary steps, including the use of armed forces" to assist any affiliates of the Southeast Asian Treaty Organization requesting defense assistance. The vote was 414–0 in the House and 88–2 in the Senate.

Years later the Senate Foreign Relations Committee held hearings questioning the information it had received from the administration on which the resolution was based. Senator William Fulbright, Chairman of the committee, told Secretary of Defense Robert McNamara:

We met, if you will recall, for 1 hour and 40 minutes, in a joint meeting of the Armed Services and this committee and we accepted your statement completely without doubt. I went on the floor to urge passage of the resolution. * * * I had no independent evidence, and now I think I did a great disservice to the Senate. I feel very guilty for not having enough sense at that time to have raised these questions and asked for evidence. I regret it. * * * If I had had enough sense to require complete evaluation I never would have made the mistake I did.[5]

The Joint Committee on Atomic Energy, which existed from 1946 until 1947, is widely accused of having been coopted by the executive branch and the nuclear industry. It was praised for years as a model of responsibility and for sharing in the making of policy. More recently, however, critics have questioned whether it was exercising sufficiently critical oversight and independent judgment over nuclear policy. One such critic said the committee had "developed such an institutional bias toward atomic energy that it [was] not able to criti-

---

[2] U.S. Congress. Committee on International Relations. Special Subcommittee on Investigations. Congress and Foreign Policy, Report, p. 3.
[3] Public Law 88–408, approved Aug. 10, 1964.
[4] Johnson, Lyndon Baines. The Vintage Point: Perspective of the Presidency, 1963–1969. New York, Holt, Rinehart and Winston, 1971, p. 115.
[5] U.S. Congress. Senate. Committee on Foreign Relations. The Gulf of Tonkin, the 1964 Incidents. Hearing on Feb. 20, 1968. Washington, U.S. Government Printing Office, 1968, pp. 80–81.

cally examine atomic energy programs."⁶ Supporters deny these charges noting that though an antinuclear movement has grown up recently, the joint committee's decisions have stood the test of time quite well. Congress abolished the committee in 1977 as part of a move to reform committee structures.

In the cases examined in the course of this study, cooptation (in the sense of precluding serious examination of a problem) is not a significant theme. Since the end of the Vietnam war, Congress has played an active and critical role in foreign policy, and the cases examined in this study were ones in which Congress showed particular interest. It is when Congress does not challenge the executive branch and accepts its information and views uncritically, whether in consultation or through any other media, that cooptation becomes a danger.

B. Differing Political Objectives and Institutional Needs

The second problem found in both branches is a difference in methods, objectives, and career needs. While it may be assumed that both branches share the ultimate goal of developing an effective foreign policy, methods of career advancement and the working principles in the two branches are different. One observer states, "The rules of the congressional game and those of the foreign policy game, however, are often contradictory, and when participants from the two arenas try to reach decisions jointly, their contrasting behavior patterns are almost certain to produce conflict, regardless of the extent of their disagreement on substance."⁷

A prime example of the different game rules between the two branches concerns secrecy. Executive officials engaged in diplomacy with foreign countries emphasize the importance of maintaining confidentiality in negotiations and their careers are likely to be enhanced by reputations for an ability to keep sensitive information from becoming public. Members of Congress, on the other hand, are more likely to emphasize the public's right to know and they may gain from finding and making public information about a possible foreign policy action. Members of Congress consider themselves as able to keep a secret as anyone else when they recognize legitimate need for secrecy. Nevertheless, executive branch officials are often reluctant to share confidential information with legislative officials. Although some executive officials concede that Members of Congress are no more likely to leak confidential information than executive officials, they contend that simply enlarging the number of people knowing such information increases the chance that it will be divulged.

The difference is a longstanding one. The need for "secrecy and dispatch" was cited by Alexander Hamilton as one of the reasons for denying the House of Representatives a share of the treatymaking power.⁸ Fear that confidential information will seep out is still one of the most frequent reasons executive branch officials cite for not consulting with Members of Congress.

---

⁶ Prepared statement of James Cubie of Congress Watch. In U.S. Congress. Senate. Temporary Select Committee To Study the Senate Committee System. Hearings on Jurisdictions, Referrals, Numbers and Sizes, and Limitations on Membership. Pt. 2, Sept. 14 and 15, 1976. Washington, U.S. Government Printing Office. 1976, p. 97.
⁷ Heginbotham, Stanley J. "Checks and Balances: The Rules of the Game," Foreign Policy, winter 1983–84.
⁸ The Federalist No. 75. Cooke, Jacob E., ed. The Federalist. Connecticut, Wesleyan University Press, 1961, p. 507.

One of the primary reasons administration officers kept Congress out of the decisions to establish diplomatic relations with China was that "news leaks of the new policy might have led to a reversal of the policy with possibly strong recriminations in American politics." [9] Executive officers contended that Chinese leaders preferred secret negotiations, and that public knowledge of the negotiations might have signaled intentions to the Soviet Union.

Secrecy was cited as the main reason President Carter did not consult with any congressional leaders prior to the attempted rescue of the U.S. hostages in Iran on April 24, 1980. The President concluded that the success of the operation and the safety of those involved depended upon total surprise and total secrecy, and that it was essential to limit the knowledge of the plan to a very small group. "He therefore concluded that it was not possible in this instance to engage in the consultations under section 3 of the War Powers Resolution." [10]

Some Members of Congress agreed with the President's decision not to consult any Members of Congress in this case, but others questioned it. Senator Charles Percy contended that consultation would have involved only a few Members of Congress, four to eight people, while hundreds of persons in the executive branch must have known about the operation. Senator Frank Church, then Chairman of the Foreign Relations Committee, said:

> I do not think that there was any genuine concern about a leak in a closely held matter of this kind with the people the President would have consulted with, whomever they may have been. We know them and there would not have been any leak.
> I rather think the reluctance to consult is that the President might have gotten advice from the Congress that he did not want to get.[11]

Senator Church continued that since the mission had failed, he had seen all kinds of information on the attempt, that the committee could not get, in the New York Times. If there was a sieve, he said, it was not Congress but downtown—the executive branch. In such situations each branch has separate, often political, interests, that stand as a barrier to effective consultation.

C. Lack of Knowledge and Understanding of the Other Branch and its Concerns

Lack of knowledge of the other branch and its concerns heightens the barrier to consultation created by differing institutional interests. The executive branch often incorrectly estimates opinion in Congress. For example, one reason the administration did not consult Congress prior to its decision to establish diplomatic relations with China at the end of 1978, a case study found, was that it "grossly overemphasized the power of the China lobby in Congress." [12] Few officials seem to know which Members might be able to give them the most insight or help in a particular problem.

In the executive branch, much of the problem stems from a continual turnover of personnel in the jobs that deal with both foreign policy

---

[9] Sutter, Robert. Executive-Legislative Consultations on China Policy, 1978–1979, p. 3.
[10] Statement of Hon. Warren Christopher, Acting Secretary of State. U.S. Congress. Senate. Committee on Foreign Relations. The Situation in Iran. Hearing, May 8, 1980. Washington, U.S. Government Printing Office, 1981, p. 4.
[11] Ibid., p. 7.
[12] Sutter, Robert. Executive-Legislative Consultations on China Policy, 1978–79, p. 24.

and legislation. Career Foreign Service officers, who often have little opportunity for dealing with Members of Congress or the legislative process because of lengthy periods of service abroad, are usually rotated to new positions after 2 or 3 years. Noncareer political appointees dealing with foreign policy are usually replaced with a change of administrations if not earlier. In the decade from 1973 to 1983, for example, there were six Secretaries of State and eight Assistant Secretaries of State for Congressional Relations and for Inter-American affairs.[13] In either event valuable knowledge and experience gained in dealing with Congress and legislation may be lost when the officials move on.

For their part, Members of Congress often appear insensitive to executive branch concerns for relations with foreign governments. Busy with their legislative and representational functions, they focus their interest in the United States and in their constituencies. Most get little opportunity for exposure to foreign countries and often are criticized when they do take trips abroad. Since international negotiations are an executive branch function, Members do not often get to observe, much less participate, in them.

D. PERSONALITY PROBLEMS

Effective consultation often depends on good personal relations between Members of Congress and their staff and executive branch officials of various levels. As suggested above, the frequent turnover in both branches, particularly the executive branch, often disrupt such relationships when they do exist. Particular personalities have also proved to be barriers to consultation.

On the executive side, some persons apparently dislike consultation, do not consider it important, or make it difficult. Henry Kissinger, respected as National Security Adviser to President Nixon and later as Secretary of State under Presidents Nixon and Ford, had a style of maintaining secrecy both from Congress and from most of his executive branch colleagues. Case studies of the SALT I (Strategic Arms Limitations Talks) Agreement and the early years of negotiations on SALT II indicate that Kissinger discouraged congressional efforts to obtain information on the policies being pursued and limited the amount of information supplied to Congress. One study reported that up to 1973 there was only one administration official—Henry Kissinger—who was competent to discuss the substance of the negotiations on strategic arms and he rarely did so.

Kissinger's briefings of Congress on SALT matters took place only on those rare occasions when the President and his assistant decided it was useful for the White House to discuss certain national security matters with Congress—in the spring of 1970 when the administration feared that monies for the Safeguard system would be cut; in the summer of 1972 when the administration sought congressional ratification of the SALT I accords; and in June 1973, prior to Chairman Brezhnev's trip to the United States.[14]

---

[13] For list of key State Department officials since 1945 see: U.S. Congress. Senate. Committee on Foreign Relations. The Senate Role in Foreign Affairs Appointments. Committee Print. Revised July 1982, pp. 109–119.
[14] Platt, Alan. The U.S. Senate and Strategic Arms Policy, 1969–1977. Boulder, Westview Press, 1978, p. 44.

The case study on the Turkish arms embargo found that several congressional and State Department sources contended that anti-Kissinger sentiment was the primary motivation for congressional action.

Yet there was far more than a clash of personalities involved. Kissinger's words and actions throughout the fall of 1974 reinforced the perception that he had little regard for Congress, for the role of consultation in making American foreign policy, and for the legal questions raised by the lawmakers.[15]

On the legislative side abrasive personalities have also sometimes made foreign policy discussions difficult. An equivalent barrier, however, has been that some Members lack interest in foreign policy issues and discourage consultative efforts by their lack of interest. Executive officials have complained that they set up meetings to discuss an issue and few Members attend, or that unless a situation is front-page news, Members just do not want to learn about it.

Personalities can also have a positive effect on consultation. Robert Straus, President Carter's Special Trade Representative, was acclaimed for facilitating congressional approval of the agreements reached in multilateral trade negotiations embodied in the Trade Agreements Act of 1979. One study concluded about Straus: "His political judgment, charismatic personality, and bipartisan rapport with Congress, particularly with the important trade legislators, are often cited as critical factors in obtaining widespread congressional approval for the MTN." [16]

Yet it can be questioned whether he would have been consulting with Congress at all if the Trade Act of 1974 had not made congressional approval of the agreements mandatory.

E. Pressure of Time

In both branches time is a factor inhibiting consultation, not primarily because of urgent crises, but because of busy schedules.

Executive officials emphasize that the need for speed in dealing with an international crisis often does not permit consultation of Congress. This study found, however, that usually the time available for making an important foreign policy decision is ample to include the consultation of Congress. Most of the situations examined during this study had been brewing over a long period of time, such as the normalization of relations with the People's Republic of China, or they continued for many years. While it is generally recognized that there could be crises, such as an attack on U.S. forces, in which an immediate Presidential decision was necessary, for the vast majority of foreign policy decisions the urgency is not that great.

The time required by consultation is a real barrier in another sense. Members of Congress have so many competing demands on their time that they feel able to spend time only on the highest priority issues. Executive branch officials are also often overloaded and look on consultation as an activity which diverts them from their "real" work of dealing with foreign countries and developing policy.

Time is a factor in a third way, that consultation almost always begins too late in the congressional view. Executive branch officials

---

[15] Laipson, Ellen. Congressional-Executive Relations and the Turkish Arms Embargo, p. 29.
[16] Ahearn, Robert. Congress and Foreign Trade Policy, p. 135.

wait to seek discussion with Congress until a decision has been made or they are committed internationally to a course that requires congressional support. Or, as in the Cyprus case or the AWACS case, they wait too long to address congressional concerns and resentment and tension in Congress grow. Similarly, Members of Congress do not indicate their interest in a problem until it has become a center of public attention by which time the executive branch may have already formed its position.

F. STRUCTURAL PROBLEMS

Both the legislative and executive branches have an intrinsic structural barrier to consultation; namely, the diffusion of decisionmaking within each branch. In Congress there is no single person or group who can speak for the whole prior to a vote; a vote is the only way that the will of Congress can be ascertained. In the executive branch often so many agencies and bureaus are involved in a decision that the process of obtaining agreement among all of them on a policy is arduous and there is extreme reluctance to multiply the difficulty by bringing Congress into it.

Frequently consultation problems are attributed to congressional reforms of the 1970's that reduced the power of the leadership and increased the powers of individual Members and subcommittees. The executive branch has claimed that it is difficult to know whom to consult, or complained that it was necessary to consult too many committees and Members. The problem is more longlasting than the past decade, since Congress is inherently a decentralized body. There can never be a single person or group in Congress who speaks for the entire Congress, as the President may for the executive branch. Moreover, as congressional consideration of problems has become more complex, consultation through committee channels has necessarily become more difficult as more committees have become involved in foreign policy problems.[17]

Although the executive branch has a hierarchical structure with a single decisionmaker at the top, the pinpointing of a single person or group for consultation on a specific issue is little easier than in Congress. On each issue consultative efforts might involve representatives of at least one substantive bureau in the Department of State, the Bureau of Congressional Relations, any number of other departments and agencies, and finally representatives of the National Security Council and White House. In recent periods when relations between the Department of State and the National Security Council have been strained, consultation limited to representatives of the Department of State has proved inadequate because the important decisions were being made in the National Security Council and the Department of State was almost as much outside the process as Congress.[18]

Neither branch has effectively developed procedures, at least on a widespread basis, that might facilitate consultation despite the diffusion of power within each branch. Congress has worked out a systematic way of getting executive branch opinion on all legislation it considers, but it often fails to find out about important foreign policy

---

[17] For further discussion, see Collier, Ellen C. Strengthening the Legislative Side.
[18] For further discussion, see Kendrick, Joseph T. Strengthening the Executive Branch Procedures.

decisions not requiring legislation. The executive branch can put on a powerful campaign of persuasion when it recognizes that essential congressional support may not be forthcoming, but unless it perceives there may be trouble with a measure in Congress, it may not undertake negotiations with Congress at all.

G. INTEREST GROUPS

Both branches must deal with the problem of interest groups. Interest groups may be either a barrier to consultation or a channel for it. They are a barrier to consultation when they add to mistrust between the branches. One perception in the executive branch creating mistrust is that Members of Congress are so parochial and vulnerable to pressure from constituent interest groups that they should not help shape foreign policy decisions affecting the national interest. With this line of reasoning, the executive branch may see the strength of a lobby as a rationale for not consulting, as was indicated by the case studies on China, the Turkish arms embargo, and arms sales.

Interest groups are a channel of communication when either branch uses them to enhance their own information and convey views to each other. They may also serve a helpful role to Congress by providing timely and frankly advocative information that is independent of the executive branch.[19]

In most cases there are interest groups on both sides of an issue, somewhat balancing each other's influence. The eventual balancing effect of lobbies on both sides was demonstrated in studies on the Rhodesian sanctions and on the AWACS sale to Saudi Arabia.

The case study on Rhodesian sanctions showed persuasive metals industry witnesses at hearings on the Byrd amendment testified in favor of the resumption of chromium imports to allow such imports despite United Nations sanctions.[20] Years later, testimony from a steel industry representative who conceded that technical changes had reduced U.S. dependence on imported chromium, helped persuade Congress to repeal the Byrd amendment. In addition, an official of the United Steelworkers of America argued that a reimposition of the sanctions would not endanger jobs in the steel industry. The executive branch found its efforts to defend the sanctions were better received where the Congressional Black Caucus was strong and active.

Similarly, in Middle East arms sales cases there have been interest groups active both for and against the sales. A study of the AWACS and F-15 enhancements package to Saudi Arabia in 1981 found: "Among the critics of the Saudi arms sale package were the American Israel Public Affairs Committee (AIPAC); Jewish War Veterans of the United States; and Americans for Democratic Action (ADA). The main interest group speaking on behalf of the Saudi sales was the National Association of Arab-Americans (NAAA). In addition, U.S. industries such as Boeing Corp. and various subcontractors who would benefit from the sales were active on behalf of the proposal."[21]

---

[19] Postbrief, Sam. Strengthening Foreign Policy Information Sources for Congress, p. 38.
[20] Copson, Raymond. Sanctions against Rhodesia, p. 21.
[21] Grimmett, Richard F. Arms Sales to Saudi Arabia: AWACS and the F-15 Enhancements. Congress and Foreign Policy, 1981, p. 43.

Both branches have sometimes used interest groups to apply pressure on the other. In June 1979, when the administration wanted to maintain the sanctions on Rhodesia longer. "Union officials and black political organizations were contacted and asked to write Members of Congress in support of the sanctions—although the staff who dealt with these letters generally recognized them as administration inspired and apparently gave them little weight." [22] The case study on the Turkish arms embargo found that Congress used the Greek-American lobby as an outside network of political support. Such activities by the executive branch are limited by a provision of law which prohibits the use of appropriated funds, without express authorization by Congress, for stimulating grass roots lobbying of Members of Congress on pending legislation or programs.[23]

In conclusion, lobbies and interest groups have emerged as a way for individuals and groups to get their messages to both the executive branch and Congress, and as one channel for persuasion between the two branches. At the same time, there have been prominent scandals involving the activities of a few foreign policy lobbies, and these serve to caution against improper activities.

---

[22] Copson, Raymond. Sanctions against Rhodesia, p. 55.
[23] Sec. 1913 of title 18, United States Code. See also: U.S. Congress, Committee on Armed Services. Investigations Subcommittee. Allegations of Improper Lobbying by Department of Defense Personnel of C-5B and B-1B Aircraft and Sale to Saudi Arabia of the Airborne Warning and Control System. Committee Print No. 24, Dec. 30, 1982. Washington, U.S. Government Printing Office, 1982, 29 pp.

PART 3. IMPROVING CONSULTATION

This part discusses measures to make consultation on foreign policy between the two branches more effective. The first chapter summarizes three functional studies which explored from various points of view the problems in improving consultation and methods of implementing various recommendations that have been made. The second chapter analyzes major options for action that have emerged.

I. THREE FUNCTIONAL STUDIES

Three studies focusing on different approaches to improving legislative-executive consultation are summarized here: (A) Strengthening Executive Branch Procedures; (B) Strengthening the Legislative Side; (C) Strengthening Foreign Policy Information Sources for Congress.

A. EXECUTIVE-LEGISLATIVE CONSULTATION ON FOREIGN POLICY: STRENGTHENING EXECUTIVE BRANCH PROCEDURES [1]

There are four major problems relating to executive branch procedures for consultation with Congress: (1) attitudes and lack of trust; (2) timing of consultation; (3) deciding whom should be consulted; and (4) organizational relationships.

1. ATTITUDES AND LACK OF TRUST

One of the most important factors inhibiting consultation is distrust of Congress within the executive branch and reluctance to involve Congress in the process of making foreign policy. Some of these attitudes stem from institutional tensions built in by the separation of powers under the Constitution, and some stem from practical problems such as pressure of time and concern for security leaks. Although Foreign Service officials have become more sensitive to the congressional role in foreign policy in the past 5 years as a result of programs aimed at improving these attitudes, renewed emphasis might be given to such efforts as [2]

—Continuing special courses within the executive branch on the role of Congress in foreign policy, and integrating this topic into other courses;
—Opening Foreign Service Institute short-term courses to congressional participants;

---

[1] Summarized from: U.S. Congress. House. Foreign Affairs Committee. Executive-Legislative Consultation on Foreign Policy: Strengthening Executive Branch Procedures. Congress and Foreign Policy Series No. 2. Committee Print, June 1981. By Joseph T. Kendrick, consultant to the Congressional Research Service. Washington, U.S. Government Printing Office, 1981, 77 pp.
[2] Ibid., p. 1.

— Expanding State Department seminars for Members of Congress and congressional staff having responsibility for an area or problem;
— Continuing special programs to provide congressional personnel a better understanding of the decisionmaking process and crisis management systems;
— Continuing the congressional fellowship program under which Foreign Service officers work for a period on Capitol Hill.

2. WHEN SHOULD CONGRESS BE BROUGHT INTO THE DECISIONMAKING PROCESS?

Congress seeks to be brought into the decisionmaking process early, but there are problems in determining how early. After a decision has been made, discussions with Congress are too late to be considered true consultation. If a problem has not developed sufficiently, it may be premature to involve Congress because there are no focal points for discussion and the options are not clear. Many argue that the optimum time for consultation on the initiative of the executive branch is, in most instances, at some point after the administration has developed various options, although the executive branch needs to signal as early as possible to the responsible congressional unit when a problem is emerging. On emerging issues prior to the formulation of options, subcommittees may be in a better position to initiate consultation through regular and systematic meetings to oversee policy in a geographic or functional area.

3. WHO SHOULD BE CONSULTED?

This is a question of strategy and tactics. Although the State Department approach of giving primacy to consulting with the two foreign affairs committees is widely approved, many Members outside the committees are often consequently offended because they had not been consulted. In addition, many other committees have jurisdiction over various foreign policy related problems. Methods by which the Department of State might extend consultation to a wider range of Congress include:
— Building coalitions of interest around significant foreign policy issues by establishing ad hoc working groups representing diverse views in both the legislative and executive branches;
— Assigning each congressional relations officer a designated number of Members for whom he would have responsibility for consultation on any topic of interest to those Members;
— Utilizing Members of Congress on a rotating basis as advisers at international negotiations;
— Continuing to use congressional relations officers to back up regional and functional bureaus;
— Taking initiatives in consulting with the congressional leadership and members of the Appropriations Committees;
— Expanding services on Capitol Hill and increasing the physical presence of State Department representatives there;
— Assisting and discussing issues with Members of Congress traveling abroad.

4. HOW SHOULD CONSULTATION BE CARRIED OUT?—ORGANIZATIONAL RELATIONSHIPS AND RESPONSIBILITIES

Too often consultation with Congress is sporadic or undertaken as an afterthought. Often the Bureau of Congressional Relations is not consulted on an issue by other parts of the State Department until late in the decisionmaking process. The Bureau of Congressional Relations is not, however, the only focal point in the executive for consulting with Congress. The regional and functional bureaus also play a role and on highly salient issues the White House assumes the key role. Options the State Department might consider to clarify and improve internal relations include:

—Issue formal instructions to staff that early consultation with Congress is a matter of policy;
—Seek authorization to raise the Assistant Secretary of Congressional Relations to the level of an Under Secretary to emphasize importance of the function;
—Establish a new unit within the Bureau of Congressional Relations to coordinate, monitor, and encourage consultation at the earliest reasonable stage;
—Place basic operational responsibility for consultation at the bureau level, with congressional relations assuming an increased coordinating role and focusing on gathering support for policy decisions;
—Assign qualified senior officers returning from abroad and awaiting assignments to the Bureau of Congressional Relations;
—Encourage bureaus to cooperate with efforts of their counterpart congressional subcommittees in early examination of issues and policy options.

The relationship between the White House and the Department of State can complicate consultation efforts. The White House sometimes becomes directly involved in reshaping issues without consultation of Congress. Problems can probably be reduced if the Department of State consults with Congress on a range of policy options and integrates the views of Congress into a draft for consideration by the President, as the White House tends to concentrate on the political effort to support the Presidential position. When the President contemplates major shifts of policy on which Congress has not been previously consulted, both the White House and the State Department may need to undertake consultations and, when a decision has become firm, campaigns of persuasion.

The author, Joseph T. Kendrick, concluded:

> Legislative-executive relations in the foreign affairs field can benefit by making a distinction between consultation and advocacy. Were the Department of State to take greater initiative in consulting Congress during the earlier phases of policy formulation, there should be less need for advocacy. * * *
>
> When the two functions of consultation and advocacy are regarded as separate operations, relationships between the two branches of Government are more likely to be channeled into building a foreign policy that has a public consensual foundation. Any administration coming to power, regardless of its political composition, must balance two contending imperatives: It must provide leadership, coherence, and direction in the making of foreign policy, yet avoid mobilizing the multiple centers of congressional power into efforts to block, divert, or delay what are seen as dangerous or misguided initiatives. The resolution of

these imperatives would arguably lie not in the vigorous selling of a unilateral executive policy but in vigorous and informed involvement of Congress in shaping and refining the direction of the policy itself.[3]

B. LEGISLATIVE-EXECUTIVE CONSULTATION ON FOREIGN POLICY: STRENGTHENING THE LEGISLATIVE SIDE [4]

A chief problem affecting consultation is lack of agreement within Congress itself on the appropriate role of Congress in foreign policy. Some Members believe the executive branch should control foreign policy and do not expect much consultation except for the purpose of building necessary legislative support. A second group sees the separation of powers as placing Congress and the executive branch in adversarial positions, with the role of Congress primarily to pass judgment on the actions planned by the executive branch. It is members of a third group—those who seek a partnership role for Congress—that are most concerned about developing consultation. Even this group does not have a unified concept of what consultation should entail. The differing perceptions and the multiple roles of Congress in foreign policy require that congressional procedures in consultation be flexible, adapted to the role Members wish Congress to play on any particular issue.

Two areas for strengthening congressional procedures for consultation are examined: (1) organizational arrangements and (2) persuading the executive branch to consult.

1. ORGANIZATIONAL ARRANGEMENTS

Executive branch officials often contend that one of the main problems in consulting Congress is uncertainty on whom to consult or the necessity of consulting so many Members. The existing structure of Congress, however, forms an effective communications network if both sides utilize it fully. This structure has four components: the subcommittees, committees, leadership, and informal groups of interested members. None of these, however, can speak for the entire Congress or guarantee to deliver the vote, the result the executive branch might like from consultation.

The subcommittees represent the most specialized groups in Congress and are best equipped to help shape many areas of policy from the beginning through systematic oversight. The House Foreign Affairs and Senate Foreign Relations Committees can add a broader foreign policy perspective to the narrower geographical or functional scope of the subcommittee. The leadership, with responsibilities in the entire range of foreign and domestic issues adds a still broader perspective and also comes the closest to being able to represent the entire Congress. Individual or groups of interested Members often offer the viewpoint of those most concerned with or affected by a particular policy.

Current organizational arrangements appear inadequate for managing issues that cross committee jurisdictional lines. Options for im-

---

[3] Executive-Legislative Consultation on Foreign Policy: Strengthening Executive Branch Procedures, pp. 71–72.
[4] Summarized from U.S. Congress. House Foreign Affairs Committee. Executive-Legislative Consultation on Foreign Policy: Strengthening the Legislative Side. Congress and Foreign Policy Series No. 5. Committee Print. By Ellen C. Collier, Specialist in U.S. Foreign Policy, Congressional Research Service. Washington, U.S. Government Printing Office, 1982, 85 pp.

proving coordination and reducing the burden of multiple meetings of executive officials with different committees include more frequent joint hearings and the establishment of informal ad hoc consultative committees comprised of representatives of all relevant committees. The establishment of interagency committees in the executive branch may provide an indication that special intercommittee groups are also needed in Congress at least for consultative purposes.

The executive branch finds it easy to use differences between the House and the Senate to strengthen its own position.

For example, it has on several occasions prevented the invoking of a legislative veto by concentrating efforts in whichever Chamber it found the most support. If it is desired to counter this executive tactical strength, regular meetings among House and Senate foreign policy committee members or staff might contribute to the development of more unified congressional positions.

Designation of a standing foreign policy group as the appropriate congressional contact point in an international emergency could expedite consultation by making it crystal clear whom the administration was expected to consult. Since a joint committee on national security has not proved feasible, an alternative might be to strengthen the tradition of consulting a less formal group comprised of the leadership and the chairman and ranking minority members of the two foreign-policy committees.

2. PERSUADING THE EXECUTIVE BRANCH TO CONSULT

Experience indicates that the executive branch rarely initiates consultation with Congress unless it is seeking legislative support. Nevertheless, Congress need not wait to be consulted. Effective consultation may be initiated by Congress itself. The interested Member, subcommittee, or committee can take the initiative in pursuing information, bringing about discussion, and offering advice, and to persist in overseeing how policies are carried out. Alternatively, they can schedule regular weekly or monthly meetings between congressional subcommittees and their executive branch counterparts. Sense-of-the-Congress resolutions offer a third way and one of the few methods whereby the entire Congress can provide advice.

Congress can be reasonably confident that its views will be taken into account only when it has power and will to affect the outcome. Such power comes primarily from legislation incorporating a congressional role, from the appropriations function, and from the requirement for Senate approval of treaties and nominations. Many in both branches believe that the President needs more flexibility in foreign policy than on domestic matters, and contend that too many legislative restrictions have been placed on him. Whatever the will of Congress on this matter, legislation can establish a congressional role and provide policy guidelines while permitting latitude to deal with unexpected developments by such measures as reporting requirements and consultation requirements.

Congress could enhance the benefit of reporting requirements by more frequently using the submitted reports as a starting point for further discussion. A requirement for an annual report on U.S. foreign policy from the President or Secretary of State could form a new basis for congressional debate of broad foreign-policy issues. Requiring additional prior notifications of carefully selected actions could provide Congress more assurance of learning about proposed actions in advance and opportunity to discuss them.

Consultation requirements have seldom been effective except when accompanied by further legislative leverage, although they do make clear the congressional expectation to be consulted. Among the factors making it easy for the executive branch to circumvent consultation requirements are that (1) most of the provisions have not been specific enough in spelling out what was meant by consultation, when it should occur, and who should be involved; and (2) often the requirements have contained loopholes such as "whenever possible" or "in every possible instance."

Legislative vetoes, requiring congressional approval or permitting congressional disapproval of a proposed measure, have been used in some areas of foreign policy, such as trade and arms transfers, to bring about consultation with Congress or changes in policy to meet the congressional view. Arguments in favor of the legislative veto were that it permitted Congress to grant more flexibility or delegate more authority than might otherwise be feasible because it gave Congress some recourse if it believed the policy was not being properly executed. In addition a vote on a legislative veto proposal provided a method for obtaining the views of the entire Congress on a proposed action. On June 23, 1983, however, in *INS* v. *Chadha* the Supreme Court ruled a legislative veto unconstitutional. It held that such legislative actions must be passed by a majority of both Houses of Congress and presented to the President for signature.

The author, Ellen C. Collier, concludes: [5]

> Congress has been most successful in bringing about consultation and helping shape foreign policy when it has passed legislation that establishes a policy or program and incorporates a future role for Congress in its implementation. The Foreign Assistance Act, the Nuclear Non-Proliferation Act, the Arms Export Control Act, and the Trade Act of 1974 all provide useful examples. In such cases a great deal of legislative-executive consultation about the initial content of the policy or program was followed by episodic, but important, consultation on specific cases or issues that arose following the initial legislation.
>
> Finally, regular, routine, and sustained interest in a foreign policy issue has often led the executive branch to continue consultations with the Member, subcommittee, or committee evincing such interest * * *

C. Strengthening Foreign Policy Information Sources for Congress [6]

Adequate information is a prerequisite for effective legislative-executive consultation, and recent congressional assertiveness in foreign policy has been aided by unprecedented access to information on foreign policy and national security issues. Congress has made great strides in assuring that necessary information is provided by its staff, the congressional support services, the executive branch, and other sources.

---

[5] Ibid., p. 75.
[6] Summarized from: U.S. Congress. House. Foreign Affairs Committee. Executive-Legislative Consultation on Foreign Policy: Strengthening Foreign Policy Information Sources for Congress. Congress and Foreign Policy Series No. 4. Committee Print. By Sam Postbrief, consultant to the Congressional Research Service. Washington, U.S. Government Printing Office, 1982, 84 pp.

The desire to maintain secrecy and confidentiality continues to be a principal barrier that limits the supply of information on foreign policy to Congress. Nevertheless, classification of information is much less frequently raised as a reason for denying information to Congress. The establishment of the intelligence committees in both Houses has provided a repository for the most sensitive material, and executive branch officials expressed confidence in their integrity and discretion. Many agree that the most serious leaks of classified information originate in the executive branch and that most Members of Congress are as trustworthy as most executive branch officials, but that just enlarging the number of people having specific information increases the risk that it will be disclosed.

The study concentrated on four areas of problems or proposals for improving foreign policy information for Congress: (1) crisis information; (2) congressional support agencies; (3) lobbies and interest groups; and (4) a parliamentary-type question period.

1. CRISIS INFORMATION CENTER

An international crisis remains the situation in which Congress has the most difficulty getting reliable, timely, and accurate information from the executive branch. Mechanisms for congressional sharing and discussing information with executive officials remain undeveloped. One option to improve the situation is the establishment of a congressional crisis information center. Such a center might help to prepare the congressional leadership for effective consultation with the executive branch, permitting them to focus on the substance of the problems and options rather than on obtaining information. It might serve to reduce mutual suspicion at a time when tensions are high.

A congressional crisis information center might perform functions such as communicating with the staffs of executive branch crisis centers, receiving messages which the executive branch believes should be brought to the attention of Congress, gathering information from independent sources, producing situation reports, compiling chronologies, and analyzing options. This might require a staff of 10 to 20 persons. The center could be attached to the leadership or housed in one of the existing support agencies.

2. CONGRESSIONAL SUPPORT AGENCIES

There are four major congressional support agencies—the Congressional Research Service, the General Accounting Office, the Congressional Budget Office, and the Office of Technology Assessment. Each has a different focus and unique contribution. Together they contain a large number of analysts in foreign policy and national security affairs, many of whom have previously served in foreign policy agencies of the executive branch. The foreign affairs components of the support agencies provide numerous services for Members of Congress and their staffs, but often the services are not well known to the congressional offices. Members and staff who are interested in foreign and national security policy will find it advantageous to familiarize themselves with the resources available in the support agencies.

The great strength of the support agencies is that they attempt to provide objective, balanced information and analyses rather than fulfill an advocacy role.

3. INTEREST GROUPS

The decentralization of the congressional committee system has multiplied the number of access points in the legislative branch available to representatives of domestic and foreign lobbies. The result has been a growing awareness of the influence that such lobbies can exert on foreign policy. Often this awareness, plus prominent scandals involving a few of the foreign policy lobbies, has been accompanied by a predominantly negative impression that a weakness of Congress in dealing with foreign policy was its susceptibility to pressures from such lobbies. But lobbies also play an important role in providing Congress with a source of timely information independent from the executive branch.

The information and open advocacy of particular viewpoints supplied by interest groups can be valuable to Members if used properly. The problem for Members is to take advantage of the information source yet to maintain a balanced and independent judgment. To insure a fair hearing of all concerned interests, Members and staffs may wish to seek exposure to more diverse interests than are currently represented.

4. THE BRITISH QUESTION PERIOD

The question period works well in the British House of Commons and in other parliamentary systems as a device to insure popular control and accountability. Its success in eliciting information, and particularly foreign-policy information, in the House of Commons, where the tradition of secrecy is deep and widely tolerated, has not been as great.

Intermittently various Members have proposed a question hour for Congress, but without success. In the American context there appears to be less need for a question hour. Executive branch officials frequently appear at committee hearings that last longer and are less constrained than the question period.

The author, Sam Postbrief, concludes: [7]

> The significantly greater information-producing resources of the U.S. Congress make this British parliamentary procedure a less promising supplement for the provision of additional data on foreign policy and national security affairs. Nevertheless, it might be useful as a method of supplying individual Members of Congress not on foreign policy committees with more direct access to senior administration officials.

---

[7] Ibid., p. 2.

II. OPTIONS FOR IMPROVING CONSULTATION

Either Congress or the executive branch could strengthen any of the four components of effective consultation: An adequate range of Members; timing that permits accommodation of congressional views; inclusion of significant issues; and attitudes that recognize the role and problems of the other branch. The executive branch could consult with a wider range of Members, and Congress could assist by providing more guidance on the Members to consult. Either branch could initiate consultations earlier and establish priorities to help focus on the most important issues. The executive branch could improve its knowledge of Congress and Congress could seek to be more sensitive to diplomatic problems.

The first part of this chapter discusses various measures that each branch might undertake to promote effective consultation on a systematic basis. The last part of the chapter deals with options for improving consultation in two special situations. First, during international crises; and second, on multidimensional issues crossing agency and committee jurisdictions.

A. OPTIONS FOR THE EXECUTIVE BRANCH

Analysis of recommendations for improving consultation reveals three approaches that the executive branch might take to improve its performance in consulting with Congress on foreign policy issues: One, policy guidelines; two, confidence building measures; and three, training, awareness, and information measures.

1. POLICY GUIDELINES

The President or Secretary of State could give an impetus to consultation by issuing guidelines for determining when and how consultation should occur.

The first element would be to make clear that consultation with Congress is authorized, encouraged, and in some cases required. Secretary of State Vance issued a memorandum in 1978 that moved in this direction. It stated as policy "to extend the full resources of the Department so as to provide Congress with the information it requires to fulfill its constitutional role in the formulation of foreign affairs." [1] Many State Department personnel believed it constituted a new mandate for greater consultation with Congress and brought about efforts to consult more effectively during his stewardship. A reaffirmation and development of such a policy by each administration could set the tone for cooperation.

---

[1] Secretary Vance's directive is printed in Kendrick, Joseph T. Strengthening Executive Branch Procedures, p. 73.

The second element would be to identify the types of issues on which consultation with Congress should be undertaken. At the present time the system is haphazard. The executive branch appears to give attention only to the immediate issue on which congressional support is needed, and the difficulty of getting support seems to be the main factor determining how much effort is expended on discussions with Congress. A policy directive could point out that consultation deserves priority status on the following types of issues:
—Programs for which legislation or appropriations are needed; e.g., foreign aid programs.
—Important treaties requiring Senate advice and consent or international agreements requiring congressional approval or implementing legislation; e.g., arms control treaties.
—Key nominations requiring Senate confirmation; e.g., the nomination of Kenneth Adelman to be Director of the U.S. Arms Control and Disarmament Agency.
—Issues on which Congress has clearly indicated its desire to be consulted; e.g., defense policy on Taiwan.
—Policies that require broad national support.

A third element would be to suggest a program of consultation that could be varied according to the importance of the issue.
Measures in such a program could include:
—Meetings with the subcommittees or committees having relevant jurisdiction over the issue, including appropriations subcommittees and committees.
—Discussions with the congressional leadership on major issues.
—Identification of and discussions with other committees, subcommittees, and individual Members having particular interest in a problem.
—Seminars or briefings open to all Members of Congress or staff.
—Background memoranda to all congressional offices explaining policies and proposals.

Finally, a policy directive on consultation might pinpoint responsibility within the Department of State for assuring that priority issues were identified and that congressional views were obtained on these issues prior to a decision. Officials suggested for this responsibility have included the Assistant Secretary of State for Congressional Relations, the Director of Policy Planning, or the Executive Secretariat.

2. CONFIDENCE-BUILDING MEASURES

A second approach the executive branch might take is to strengthen programs aimed at building trust and mutual confidence between the two branches. This requires making new opportunities for members of one branch to develop effective working relations with the people and problems of the other branch. Measures in such a program might include:
—Strengthening personnel exchange programs, including the detail of Foreign Service Officers to congressional offices and the participation of congressional staff in executive branch training programs.
—Hiring people with experience in the congressional offices.

— Establishing permanent offices on Capitol Hill for congressional liaison officers to expedite constituent services.[2]
— Making available Foreign Service Officers to discuss issues with Members of Congress and staff on request.
— Increasing assistance to Members of Congress in preparing for and while on trips abroad.

3. TRAINING, AWARENESS, AND INFORMATION PROGRAMS

The third approach is to increase knowledge and understanding in the executive branch, particularly the Department of State, about Congress and the congressional role in foreign policy. Too few officials have the knowledge of interests and power centers in Congress that lobbyists for private groups find essential. Measures to promote such knowledge and greater awareness of Congress include:
— More comprehensive Foreign Service Institute courses on the role of Congress in foreign policy.
— More discussion of relevant legislation and congressional views in courses on foreign policy issues and geographic areas.
— Better tracking of views of Members and committees on foreign policy.
— Wider dissemination of literature on Congress such as the Congressional Record.

B. OPTIONS FOR CONGRESS

The study has indicated that Congress can promote more effective consultation by providing the executive branch an incentive to consult and developing procedures to facilitate more timely and broader discussion of foreign policy issues. The analysis has shown four approaches Congress might consider: 1) Legislation to improve information mechanisms; (2) legislation to provide leverage; (3) consultative meetings; and (4) initiative in pursuing information and proposing solutions.

1. LEGISLATION TO IMPROVE INFORMATION MECHANISMS

Already Congress has assured itself a great deal of information on foreign policy issues through the addition of reporting requirements in legislation. Sometimes the legislation calls for prior notification of or consultation on certain actions. The assumption is that if Congress is informed in advance of an action, it can protest or take legislative action against any action it opposes.

Despite the large number of required reports submitted to Congress and the provisions calling for consultation with Congress, however, often the requirements have not proved effective in starting effective discussions between the two branches. There are three ways that the existing network of reporting and consultation requirements might be strengthened.

The first is by tightening existing provisions to make them more effective in bringing about consultation. Steps that might be helpful include:

---
[2] Percy, Charles H. The Partisan Gap. Foreign Policy, Winter 1981–82, p. 11.

— Specifying the committees or Members and executive branch officials to be involved; e.g. the Refugee Act of 1980 specified designated Cabinet-level officials and members of the Judiciary Committees.
— Specifying when the consultation is to occur; e.g. the Refugee Act provides that relevant information is to be supplied to the committees two weeks in advance of the consultations that are required before certain Presidential decisions.
— Specifying what constitutes consultation; e.g. the Refugee Act provides for discussions in person and that public hearings are to be held with the substance of the consultations to be printed in the Congressional Record as soon as possible.

The second way to improve the network is by filling in gaps in the legislative framework for foreign policy. Existing legislation does not establish reporting or consultation requirements in every field. Sometimes there is no legislation on a subject so there is no appropriate vehicle for congressional action. Gaps at the present time include:

— Security classification of information. Classification and declassification are currently regulated by executive order. Several Members and committees have proposed that security classification be regulated by legislation, but executive officials are hesitant to open access to secret information to all Members and staff of Congress.
— Foreign policy as a whole. There is no legislation setting a comprehensive framework for the conduct of foreign policy or for the substance of foreign policy, and no regular assessment of overall U.S. foreign policy. As a start toward this, one proposal is to require an annual report on foreign policy by either the President or the Secretary of State along the lines of the annual economic report or the "State of the World" report issued by President Nixon. Although some believe the proposal has merit, others contend the product would not be worth the time and work involved.

The third way is for committees to utilize required reports to initiate discussions whenever the material in the reports warrants. Methods that might be employed include:

— Systematic monitoring of required reports to ensure that the reports are submitted on time and contain the required information.
— Acknowledging reports and programs that fully comply with the requirements.
— Holding oversight hearings when the reports raise questions about a policy or program.

2. MEASURES TO PROVIDE LEVERAGE

The best incentive for consultation has proven to be congressional power to prevent the executive branch from undertaking an action or program without it consent.

Congress automatically has a share in decisions when appropriations are necessary, as in the case of foreign assistance legislation and the functioning of the State Department, Arms Control and Disarmament Agency, and U.S. Information Agency. The requirement for funding serves as an inducement to consultation. Similarly, the requirement for the advice and consent of the Senate to treaties provides an inducement to consult.

On many foreign-policy decisions, however, the executive branch is able to act without any further authorization or appropriation of funds, and on these issues there is no incentive for the administration to consult Congress. To correct this situation on major issues, Congress adopted legislation requiring congressional concurrence or permitting congressional disapproval of many foreign-policy decisions, including the following:
—Introduction of troops into hostilities (War Powers Resolution).
—Exercise of emergency authorities (International Emergency Economic Powers Act and National Emergencies Act).
—Arms transfers (Arms Export Control Act).
—Sale or transfer of nuclear materials (Nuclear Non-proliferation Act).
—Trade legislation (Tariff Act of 1930, Trade Act of 1974, and Trade Agreements Act of 1979).

On June 23, 1983, in *INS* v. *Chadha*, the Supreme Court ruled a legislative veto provision in the Immigration and Nationality Act unconstitutional. The Court held that such legislative actions must be bicameral and presented to the President for signature, thus invalidating vetoes by a single House or concurrent resolution, but not those by a joint resolution or bill signed by the President. Since both kinds are found in foreign-policy legislation, each piece of legislation must be scrutinized to determine the effect of the ruling.

The legislative veto mechanism was not always effective in bringing about advance consultation. Actions took place under both the War Powers Resolution and the Arms Export Control Act in which Members complained about inadequate consultation of Congress. Nevertheless, there was a general consensus that the measures served as a restraint on executive branch action and that if the provisions had not existed there would have been even less consideration of the opinion of Congress.

Moreover, Congress as a whole had been unwilling to invoke a legislative veto on a foreign-policy issue, although it had come close to doing so. A resolution of disapproval was passed in the Houe but defeated in the Senate both in regard to the shipment of nuclear fuel to India and in the AWACS sale to Saudi Arabia. As mentioned earlier, there is a reluctance among many Members of Congress to overrule the President in a major foreign-policy confrontation.

From a consultation point of view, the invoking of a veto would have meant the device had failed in the major purpose of bringing about discussion and accommodation of congressional views prior to the final decision.

Since a legislative veto by a single House or concurrent resolution has been declared unconstitutional, Congress could consider the following options:
—Requiring approval of a proposed action by joint resolution that would require signature by the President.
—Informal arrangements under which the executive branch would give great weight to the objections of key committees to planned actions, as in the case of reprogramming of foreign aid appropriations, in order to maintain the legislative authority for such actions.
—Withdrawing authorizations that were subject to and contingent on the veto and delegating powers to the President more narrowly.

—Putting new emphasis on report-and-wait and more specific consultation requirements, with a willingness to revoke authority if the requirements were not met.
—Establishing priority procedures to consider legislation disapproving proposed actions, recognizing that it might be vetoed by the President, with the anticipation that passage by a majority of both Houses might influence the President or that the veto might be overridden.

3. MORE EFFECTIVE CONSULTATIVE MEETINGS

A distinction needs to be made between formal hearings and consultation meetings and new emphasis placed on the latter. Both offer an opportunity for an entire committee or subcommittee to discuss an issue with the appropriate executive branch officials. Public hearings, however, are sometimes not satisfactory for consultation purposes. Often they are of an educational nature, with members primarily in the role of questioners and the purpose to make information available for the public. Sometimes they are posturing sessions on controversial issues with each side trying to present its case for political benefit.

A number of methods might be attempted to convert meetings from information gathering sessions into consultative sessions.

One way is to designate clearly that a certain meeting is for consultative purposes and therefore is to be a two-way exchange of views. At the present time administration witnesses are often concentrated at the beginning of a study or investigation of a situation, before committee members have had an opportunity to hear a discussion of the issues. As a result, most of the time is necessarily spent in briefing or "educating" the members. Committees could add to these briefing or informational hearings a meeting near the end of the study, perhaps just prior to the issuance of a committee report on the subject, with the purpose of presenting and discussing the views of committee members with the administration.

A second way is to focus meetings on options. This study has indicated that the prime time for consultation was probably after the options had been formulated but before a decision had been made.[3] At a consultative meeting on options, administration officials could present the options it was considering and the advantages and disadvantages it saw in each option, much as they do for the President or Secretary of State. Members of the committee could then add their views, including suggestions for additional options. By regularly requesting a consultative meeting to discuss the options under consideration, committees would increase the likelihood that their views be heard prior to the making of the decision.

A third way is to follow through with oversight meetings. Follow-through and long-term oversight is essential if Congress is to play a meaningful role in shaping policy. Foreign policy is not usually made by a single decision but the accumulation of decisions over many years. Controversy over sanctions against Rhodesia went on for 14 years. Turkish troops that intervened in Cyprus in 1974, resulting in the congressional imposition and later lifting of an arms embargo to Tur-

---
[3] See Kendrick, Joseph T., Strengthening Executive Branch Procedures.

key, still remain on the island. Congress has been trying to increase its influence or arms transfers generally since the 1960's. Thus consultation cannot be a one-time occurrence but must be sustained over a long period if Congress wishes to influence policy. Occasional or regular oversight hearings may be necessary for years if Members are to stay abreast of developments and continue to advise on how a policy or program is being carried out.

A fourth step is to use oversight meetings to identify new issues of interest to Congress. One of the most successful ways in which Congress has encouraged routine consultation has been for subcommittees or committees to hold regular oversight hearings or informal meetings with executive branch officials to review the subjects within its jurisdiction. For example, the House Foreign Affairs Subcommittee on Europe and the Middle East holds an informal meeting once a week with appropriate officials from the State Department Bureau of European Affairs and Bureau of Near Eastern and South Asian affairs to review the various problems of a particular region, such as Northern Europe. It takes almost an entire year to cover the entire area under the subcommittee's jurisdiction, but the method provides a systematic survey and insures that none of the regions is ignored by the committee. Such routine consultation builds up the background knowledge of subcommittee or committee members. It permits them to become acquainted with the officials responsible for policy in the area and encourages an interchange of views. In addition, it serves as a screening device for detecting issues deserving higher priority consultation.

Thus, there can be a cycle of consultative meetings. The cycle starts when Congress indicates its interest in a subject by holding meetings aimed initially at gathering information. It continues with additional hearings or meetings to discuss options and advise the administration of congressional views. After a decision is made, oversight meetings provide a vehicle for consultation on the carrying out of the policy. In addition, regular oversight meetings may reveal new issues that Congress wishes to address, thus starting the cycle again.

4. INITIATIVES IN PURSUING INFORMATION AND PROPOSING SOLUTIONS

Whatever the system for securing consultation in general, the influence of Congress on any particular issue depends upon the action that legislators take upon that issue. Their vigor and persistence and the quality of their contribution are often the main factors in determining whether the executive branch listens to Congress.

Committee consideration of legislation proposing solutions, programs, or policies is one way that Members of Congress have been able to get the executive branch to take their views seriously. When the executive branch is convinced that Congress may pass legislation prescribing a certain course of action, it springs into action immediately to stop or have a share in shaping such legislation. The result is often that the executive branch succeeds in stopping the proposed legislation. One former Assistant Secretary of State explained this by saying that "Nothing concentrates the mind of Congress like the awareness that they'll be reponsible for the results of their actions." [4] It might

---

[4] Atwood, Brian. New York Times, Sept. 28, 1980, p. E5.

also be said that nothing concentrates the mind of the executive branch like awareness that Congress is enacting legislation affecting foreign policy. In any event, imminent legislation results in discussions on the issues.

Travel abroad is a second way that Members of Congress can take initiatives to gain firsthand information, add to their background knowledge on a problem, and directly or indirectly through the press gain the ear of executive branch officials. Congressional trips have been important in shaping the congressional role in the Middle East, the SALT talks, and the Panama Canal treaties. In addition, since arrangements for trips are usually made by the Department of State or Defense, they provide an opportunity for interaction between congressional and executive personnel that may improve mutual understanding.

Executive branch officials have mixed views about congressional trips. Occasionally a Member of Congress visiting a foreign country states an opinion that is at variance with the President's position or that somehow causes embarrassment. The people in the foreign country may become angry or confused over U.S. policy, and the U.S. Embassy is left to smooth over the problem. Embassy officials may also find congressional visits a burden on their funds and schedules. On the other hand, some executive officials believe that foreign travel is one of the best ways that Members can broaden their understanding of foreign policy and of particular issues.

C. Options for Congress in Improving Crisis Consultation

It is during international crises, when the national security of the United States may most depend on the decisions made, that complaints of lack of consultation have been greatest in the past. During crises the executive branch often holds a monopoly on information and instruments for action that give it the means to act without consultation, authorization, or appropriations from Congress. Since the executive branch has little incentive to change current practice, Congress may wish to find ways to increase consultation. Three options are discussed below: one, designating in advance a crisis consultation group; two, establishing a congressional crisis information center; and three, tightening the consultation requirements in the War Powers Resolution.

1. Designate in Advance a Crisis Consultation Group

At the present time there is no congressional directive to the President advising him on whom he should consult when a crisis occurs. If he consults, the President may choose representatives of the leadership and certain committees, or he may select members whom he believes have the most power to persuade other members, or he may select members with whom he feels most comfortable. Members of Congress may not know whether the President is consulting with anyone at all and may assume that someone else is being consulted.

One option is to specify, formally or informally, a congressional group to serve as the point of contact between the two branches in the event of a crisis. Formally, Congress might designate by resolution or legislation appropriate committees of Congress, the chairmen and ranking minority members of such committees, the leadership of both Houses and the chairmen and ranking minority members of specified committees, or any other combination of members, and spell out the functions of the group. Informally, Congress might insist that in an international crisis the President follow a growing tradition and immediately consult with the majority and minority leaders in the Senate and the corresponding leaders in the House and the chairman and ranking minority members of the Foreign Affairs and Foreign Relations Committees. In either case, Congress would reduce the discretion of the executive branch, a loss of flexibility that the executive branch might resist.

As the crisis continues, the leadership or the initial consultative group could substitute or add other members such as the chairmen or representatives of other committees or subcommittees particularly concerned. It might be noted that during the Iranian crisis, the chairmen of the Middle East Subcommittees who had been dealing with the problem previously and would be in the future, were not included in the consultation groups.

Another option would be the establishment of a Joint Committee on National Security or separate Senate and House National Security Committees. In 1975, the Commission on the Organization of the Government for the Conduct of Foreign Policy recommended the establishment of such a joint committee for similar purposes and to receive and analyze reports submitted under the war powers resolution.

One of the chief obstacles to the Joint Committee on National Security has been the inherent difficulty in operating joint bodies. This might be resolved by establishing separate Senate and House committees. Jurisdictional concerns of existing committees might possibly be alleviated by making the new committees consultative only, with no legislative functions. Nevertheless, such concerns remain a major barrier.

2. ESTABLISH A CONGRESSIONAL CRISIS INFORMATION CENTER

A second approach is aimed at improving the information that Congress receives in a crisis. During serious foreign policy or national security crises, Congress has repeatedly experienced difficulty in getting sufficient, accurate, and timely information. This was demonstrated in the Dominican Republic intervention in 1965, the Mayaguez incident in 1975, and the Iranian hostage rescue attempt in 1980, to name only a few examples. Having little information beyond that available in the media, Members of Congress enter discussions with executive branch officials on an unequal footing. Most of the time must be spent with executive officials in effect briefing Members of Congress and bringing them up to date.

One analyst of the problem has suggested consideration of a Congressional Crisis Information Center as a method of keeping Congress better informed during a crisis.[5] The center would not seek to duplicate the information-gathering facilities of the executive branch, but it would be a central point for receiving information from the executive branch and other sources, compiling chronologies, reports, and analyses

---

[5] Postbrief, Sam. Strengthening Foreign Policy Information Sources for Congress.

of the data independently from the executive branch, and distributing it to the appropriate Members of Congress and committees. The size of the staff contemplated was between 10 and 20 individuals, drawn from present committee or support agency staff.

The purpose of a Crisis Information Center would be to allow Members and committees to obtain as much information as possible from a congressional source so that discussions with executive officials could focus on the options rather than constitute briefing sessions. The center would provide a fixed point on Capitol Hill, in place before the crisis occurs, responsible for collecting information. The executive branch could use it to transmit information more efficiently, and the leadership could use it to prepare for consultative meetings.

One of the major decisions in establishing such a center would be its location within the congressional system. Choices would include management and control by the House and Senate Intelligence Committees, the Foreign Relations and Foreign Affairs Committees, the Armed Services Committees, the congressional leadership, or one of the existing support agencies.

3. TIGHTEN CONSULTATION PROVISIONS IN WAR POWERS RESOLUTION

The crises that are of greatest concern to Congress are those that may involve the use of U.S. Armed Forces and relate to its power under the Constitution to declare war. Congress took major action to require consultation in situations that might lead to involvement in hostilities by passing, over the President's veto, the War Powers Resolution of 1973. Despite some success perhaps in restraining Presidents in the use of armed force, the War Powers Resolution does not appear to have significantly increased consultation with Congress. Presidents have continued to make unilateral decisions to send Armed Forces befor informing Congress and seeking to obtain congressional support. A possible exception is the Multinational Force and Observers (MFO) established for peacekeeping in the Sinai in 1981, for which President Reagan obtained formal congressional authorization.

Can the War Powers Resolution be made more effective in insuring that the President consults with Congress prior to deciding to send troops abroad in times of hostilities? What can Congress do, especially in view of the Supreme Court's decision in *INS* v. *Chadha?* The decision would appear to invalidate section 5(c), permitting Congress by concurrent resolution to direct the withdrawal of U.S. Armed Forces engaged in hostilities outside the United States without a declaration of war or other congressional authorization, although not section 5(b) requiring enactment of an authorization for the troops to remain beyond 60–90 days. On September 29, 1983, Congress passed the Multinational Force in Lebanon Resolution that, consistent with section 5(b) of the War Powers Resolution, authorized continued participation in the multinational force for 18 months.

One approach is to require congressional authorization for the use of troops abroad except in specified circumstances such as an attack on the United States or the rescue of U.S. citizens. The requirement for prior congressional authorization would assure consultation by making the decision to send troops a joint one. This approach was embodied in the war powers bill originally passed by the Senate in 1972. On

September 29, 1983, three Senators introduced an amendment to the War Powers Resolution (S. 1906) that would return to such prior restraints.[6]

Many observers feel this type of amendment to the war powers resolution at the present time is not feasible. Objections to the proposal have included that a requirement for prior congressional authorization might be unconstitutional or make it impossible for the President to act quickly enough in an emergency, or that a list of exceptions to the requirement would give the President carte blanche in those situations.

Another approach is to strengthen the current consultation requirement by making it more specific. At the present time the resolution states:

> The President in every possible instance shall consult with Congress before introducing United States Armed Forces into hostilities or into situations where imminent involvement in hostilities is clearly indicated by the circumstances, and after every such introduction shall consult regularly with the Congress until United States Armed Forces are no longer engaged in hostilities or have been removed from such situations.[7]

One possible change would be to specify the Members of Congress whom the President is to consult. The original resolution as reported by the House Foreign Affairs Committee required the President to consult with "the leadership and appropriate committees of Congress," but the conference committee changed this to simply "Congress," allowing the President to decide how many and which Members to consult. Proposed amendments have suggested that the consultation include but not be limited to the Senate and House leadership, and the Chairman and Ranking Minority Member of the Foreign Affairs, Foreign Relations, and Armed Services Committees. Perhaps Congress could designate such a group without formal amendment of the resolution.

A second possible change would be to broaden the instances in which the President is required to consult to cover all situations in which a President is required to report. Under the present wording, the President is required to consult only under one set of circumstances: the introduction of troops into hostilities or imminent hostilities. These are the same circumstances listed in section 4(a)(1), which triggers the provision requiring authorizing legislation for the troops to remain beyond 60 to 90 days. Thus Presidents have been reluctant to designate situations as hostilities or situations of imminent hostilities. Consultation is not currently required for cases when forces are introduced into foreign territory while equipped for combat (sec. 4(a)(2)) or in numbers which substantially enlarge U.S. forces equipped for combat already in a foreign nation (sec. 4(a)(3)).

A third option would be to clarify what is meant by the word "consult." On several occasions the executive branch has held that the President met the consultation requirement because he notified Congress prior to the actual introduction of troops. After the *Mayaguez* crisis.

---

[6] For a history of the War Powers Resolution, see U.S. Congress. House. Committee on Foreign Affairs. The War Powers Resolution. A special study of the Committee on Foreign Affairs, by John H. Sullivan. Washington, U.S. Government Printing Office, 1982, 291 pp. See also Sterling-Conner, Enid. The War Powers Resolution: Does it make a difference? In Abshire, David, and Ralph Nurnberger. The Growing Power of Congress. Beverly Hills, Sage Publication, 1981, p. 298.
[7] Public Law 93-148.

some Members of Congress introduced amendments to replace the words "seek the advice and counsel of Congress before ordering such introduction of the United States Armed Forces." [8]

Some doubt that amendments tightening the war powers resolution could be passed as a President could veto them. Others are reluctant to open the resolution to amendment for fear that it might be repealed or weakened. Another group remains unconvinced that the war powers resolution is a prudent mechanism for inclusion in the national security decision system.

D. OPTIONS ON MULTIDIMENSIONAL ISSUES

In addition to crises, a second area meriting special attention is policy made on complex issues falling into the jurisdiction of more than one executive agency or congressional committee. These include policies relating to national security and a growing number of economic, social, and scientific matters. Consultation between the two branches, like policymaking within each branch, immediately becomes more complicated whenever several bureaucratic or committee interests must be reconciled.

Although coordination of multidisciplinary problems is weak in both branches, the executive branch has a considerable advantage over Congress in dealing with such problems. As the head, the President can direct the formation of an interagency committee or task force and make a decision when there are disagreements among agencies. Even so it is often extremely difficult to reach agreement on a policy, one of the factors that make the executive branch reluctant to bring Congress into the process.

In Congress a good system has not yet developed for handling questions crossing committee jurisdictions. Multiple referrals are allowed but have often failed to be acted on and have rarely been successful in bringing about cooperation among committees in acting on mutual problems.[9] Joint hearings among committees of the same House are uncommon, and joint hearings between the Senate and the House are virtually nonexistent. The party policy committees and leadership serve as the primary coordinating mechanisms for issues overlapping committees, but as they deal with all issues they cannot concentrate on one problem over a long period of time like an interagency group or task force.

Often interdisciplinary problems affect many countries so solutions are sought through multilateral channels such as international organizations or conferences. Examples are narcotics control, promotion of trade, prevention of terrorism, protection of the environment and oceans, and refugee problems.

Congress often finds it difficult to influence U.S. policy in an international organization or conference. The executive branch as the negotiator may agree to a course of action (such as the imposition of sanctions against Rhodesia) or a financial commitment (such as the

---

[8] H.R. 7594, 94th Congress.
[9] In the 96th Congress, approximately 10 percent of the bills referred to the Foreign Affairs Committee were referred jointly to other committees. Of the 82 foreign affairs bills or resolutions jointly referred, 23 had action taken by more than one committee, and four were enacted.

amounts to replenish the funds of an international development bank) and then contend that congressional concurrence is essential for the United States to live up to its international obligations. Or, if Congress suggests a modification, the executive branch points out that any change would require renegotiation by a large number of nations and endanger the whole agreement. Congress may have to choose between endorsing an agreement it does not like and preventing completion of a laboriously achieved agreement.

Following are options for improving consultation between the executive branch and Congress on multidisciplinary issues.

1. ESTABLISH AD HOC CONSULTATIVE COMMITTEES

The leadership could designate groups for consultative, not legislative, purposes. Such committees could be comprised of representatives of all the committees having jurisdiction over some aspect of the problems or individual Members with a particular interest in the question. Their purpose would be to hold consultative meetings with executive branch officials to discuss guidelines and goals for international negotiations. In addition, the committee could monitor the progress of the negotiation. As the negotiations neared completion, the committee could be a channel of communication among the various congressional committees involved as well as with the executive branch.

2. STRENGTHEN PRACTICE OF HAVING CONGRESSIONAL OBSERVERS INVITED TO ALL IMPORTANT INTERNATIONAL NEGOTIATIONS

The practice has been growing ever since the Treaty of Versailles was defeated by the Senate, but there are still important conferences in which there are no congressional observers. Attendance at conferences gives Members the opportunity to learn firsthand of the problems involved and to discuss issues and options with the American negotiators.

3. INSIST ON SENATE CONFIRMATION OF NEGOTIATORS

Senate confirmation of the head of the American delegation negotiating an important treaty provides an opportunity to discuss the purpose of the proposed treaty at the outset. To serve this purpose, Senators need to learn as much as possible about the proposed negotiations prior to the confirmation hearing so that they can provide advice on goals at that time. In any event, hearings on the nomination help establish a relationship between the Senate Foreign Relations Committee and the negotiator, laying the groundwork for subsequent consultative meetings.

4. FORM INFORMAL CAUCUSES OF INTERESTED MEMBERS

A fourth option is for interested members from various committees to form informal caucuses on issue in which they are particularly interested. Although they would have no formal standing or role in the legislative process, such groups have provided a way to become informed, discuss issues with executive branch officials, and to attempt to influence executive branch decisions and legislation.

E. CONCLUSION

None of the options discussed above could guarantee effective consultation between the two branches. Adoption of some of them might, however, contribute to the development of a system to identify priority issues and appropriate persons for consultation in a timely manner. The individual measures might be modest but nonetheless might help to institutionalize processes encouraging effective consultation.

Some observers have called for a more general approach to improving foreign policy consultation and the relationship between the two branches. Warren Christopher, Deputy Secretary of State from 1977 to 1981, has advocated a compact between the executive and Congress on foreign policy decisionmaking.[10] He has suggested that the concept of the compact be considered by a special hearing of the Senate Foreign Relations Committee or the House Foreign Affairs Committee, or that one of the institutes dedicated to foreign affairs draw together a group of scholars and public officials to probe the idea and discuss implementation. An agreement on consultation might be an important part of such a compact.

Another study of legislative-executive relations in foreign policy also concluded that a "clearer sense of a division of labor in the diplomatic field by officials on both ends of Pennsylvania would go far toward achieving the goal of a more unified, stable, and successful American approach to external problems in the years ahead." [11]

Efforts to increase understanding of the proper roles of Congress and the President in foreign policy might be beneficial in improving attitudes and could influence policymakers in the executive branch and Congress for a time.

The persistence of the nonconsultation problem, however, suggests that there is no permanent solution. The quality and quantity of consultation will continue to depend on the relationship and efforts of each successive President and Congress.

---

[10] Christopher, Warren. Ceasefire Between the Branches: A Compact in Foreign Affairs. Foreign Affairs, summer 1982.
[11] Crabb, Cecil V., Jr., and Pat M. Holt. Invitation to Struggle. Congress, the President and Foreign Policy. Washington, Congressional Quarterly Press, 1980, p. 218.